seventeen presents...

500

Health &
Fitness Tips

Library of Congress Cataloging-in-Publication Data
Seventeen 500 health & fitness tips.
    p. cm.
  ISBN 978-1-58816-768-2
  1. Teenagers--Health and hygiene. 2. Teenagers--Nutrition. 3.
Physical fitness for youth--Juvenile literature. I. Seventeen. II. Title:
Seventeen 500 health and fitness tips. III. Title: Seventeen five
hundred health & fitness tips.
  RA777.S45 2009
  613'.0433--dc22
                                                        2009011420

Published by Hearst Books
A Division of Sterling Publishing Co., Inc.
387 Park Avenue South, New York, NY 10016

Seventeen is a trademark of Hearst Communications, Inc.

www.seventeen.com

For information about custom editions, special sales, premium and
corporate purchases, please contact Sterling Special Sales
Department at 800-805-5489 or specialsales@sterlingpub.com.

Distributed in Canada by Sterling Publishing
c/o Canadian Manda Group, 165 Dufferin Street
Toronto, Ontario, Canada M6K 3H6

Distributed in Australia by Capricorn Link (Australia) Pty. Ltd.
P.O. Box 704, Windsor, NSW 2756 Australia

Manufactured in China
Sterling ISBN 978-1-58816-768-2

seventeen presents…

500

Health & Fitness Tips

HEARST BOOKS
A division of Sterling Publishing Co., Inc.

New York / London
www.sterlingpublishing.com

contents

005

hi!

Consider this the **ultimate guide** to getting healthy. We've given you inside access to the top **celeb** trainers and the latest advice on what to eat whenever and wherever you are, so you'll always look and feel your best.

—the editors of *seventeen*

008

get fit now!

Getting in shape can be **intimidating**—it's hard to know what moves are best for you—but we've done all the work for you with these 32 **fun**, fast workouts. Just choose your moves and you'll start to see a **tighter, toned-up** you in no time!

17 FYI

Choose your favorite workouts in this section and do them up to 5 times a week. There are plenty to choose from, so you'll never get bored!

A "rep" means doing a move once (parts a and b). A "set" means doing all the moves shown in one workout one time through.

the beginner's workout

Whether you're a fitness pro or new to exercise, Harley Pasternak's routine is a great basic workout you can do anywhere, anytime! Best part? You can do the whole thing in just 25 minutes, busy girl!

If you're a **beginner** (new to exercise), do 2 sets of these moves 2 days a week, plus 5 minutes of cardio (anything that gets your heart rate up, like biking or jogging) before and after the workout.

If you're **advanced** (you exercise at least 3 times a week), do 3 sets of these moves 3 days a week, with 5 minutes of cardio to warm up and 10–15 minutes of cardio afterward at a higher intensity.

You'll need a set of 3-pound weights.

#1 walk-lunge

a. Lunge forward with your left foot. Make sure your left knee doesn't go past your left ankle. Always keep your back upright, your head straight, and look forward.

b. Come up, but don't stop—immediately bring right foot forward and lunge with your right leg. Take 20 steps on each leg.

a.

b.

This works your BUTT and LEGS!

a. This tones your ARMS and CHEST!

b.

#2 kitchen-counter push-up

a. Stand with both feet and hands shoulder-width apart. Place hands on the edge of a counter or desk, keeping body straight as a board.

b. Slowly lower yourself down, with eyes on the surface of the counter or desk. Push yourself back up. Go down and up 20 times total.

#3 seated dumbbell row

a. Sit with your feet planted and lean slightly forward (keep tummy tight and back straight). Hold a 3-pound weight in each hand.

b. As you exhale, draw your elbows straight back, so you feel your shoulder blades pinch. Inhale as you lower arms down. Do 20 reps.

a.

This sculpts your ARMS and upper BACK!

b.

a.

This will give you killer ABS!

#4 reverse crunch

a. Lie on your back with palms flat on the floor at your side. Bend your knees and tuck your heels into your butt.

b. Use your ab muscles to roll your knees toward your chest, lifting your tailbone. Do 20 times.

b.

#5

don't give up

If you just started and find it hard to stay committed, keep going! Experts say it takes 21 days to turn a new activity into habit—that's just three weeks until you're saying, "I can't wait to work out!"

#6
notice the mind games

About halfway through your workout, it's normal to start thinking about stopping. You might even hear a voice that tries to talk you out of finishing, saying things like, "You're tired," or, "It won't matter if you don't finish the last 15 minutes." Instead of giving in, try to talk back. Say, "I hear you, but we're finishing." Recognizing that all it is—just a voice—will help take the power out of it, and make it easier to keep going.

get awesome legs!

Feel hot in short shorts and mini-skirts with the help of Fergie's trainer, **Natasha Kufa.** You'll tone up your legs and get fit in no time!

You'll need 3-pound weights and a resistance band.

Warm up by doing 10 minutes of cardio (running, walking). Leg muscles need time to rest so do one set of these moves just **twice** a week, and stretch after. On other days, do **20 to 30** minutes of cardio to stay fit. You should see a noticeable difference after one month!

a.

b.

#7 straight-leg dead lift

a. Stand with a weight in each hand. Bend at the waist until your upper body is parallel to the floor; let the weights travel down your thighs.

b. Reverse the movement, inching the weights back up your thighs as you clench your thigh muscles. Repeat 20 times.

Go slow to maximize results. Count 4 seconds while lowering and three to come up. This works your hamstrings and lower back.

#8
chair pose

Squat down and lift arms up in a goal post position. Keep your back **straight**, abs **tucked in**, and your neck in line with your spine. Hold for 30 seconds and then slowly rise back up.

You can lean against a wall if this is too hard.

#9 squat & leg lift

a. With your feet hip-width apart and a resistance band around your ankles for extra intensity, slowly lower into a squat.

b. Keeping weight centered, slowly stand and lift leg out. Bring it down; repeat with other leg. Do 20 on each side.

a.

b.

Tones every bit of your THIGHS.

#10 knee kicks

a. Lie on your side with bottom leg bent. Begin with top leg straight, and then bend that knee toward floor.

b. Kick your top leg back into the position you started from (so that it's straight). Do this 20 times on each leg.

a.

b.

Feel the burn on your OUTER LEG.

stretches

Stretching improves flexibility. Try to hold each pose until your muscles loosen up (30–60 seconds).

#11
triangle pose

#12
downward-facing dog

#13
the pigeon

get amazing abs!

Get hardcore abs fast with these insider secrets from Shakira's trainer, **Bobby Strom!**

You'll need 3-pound weights and a medicine ball or a soccer ball.

To tone your abs, do one set of these moves **5 times** a week. Always make sure to suck in your **lower stomach** and contract your **abs** as you do each exercise. Lift up using your ab muscles to avoid straining your neck, legs, or upper back.

a.

Great for
your entire
MIDSECTION!

b.

#14
cross knee lifts

a. Using a sturdy table or the steps on a staircase, get into a plank position, placing hands slightly more than shoulder-width apart. Stand on balls of feet.

b. Lift knee across stomach, turning hips (knee should go toward opposite shoulder). Repeat on other side to complete one rep. Do 20 reps.

#15 leg lifts

a. Sit on the edge of a chair with knees bent and a soccer ball or stack of books at your feet. Raise your knees up, bringing your feet off the floor.

b. Use your abs to lift legs up and over the ball, never letting feet touch the floor. To complete one rep, return feet to position A. Do 6 reps.

a.

Flattens your lower ABS and shapes your curves.

b.

#16 knee-to-elbow lifts

a. Lie on a mat or towel, with left hand behind head. Bend knees; place feet flat on floor.

b. Use your abs to lift left elbow to right knee (don't just turn elbow in). Do 15 on each side.

a.

b.

Feel it in your LOWER ABS and SIDES.

a.

#17 curl-ups

a. Sit on the floor, hands flat and slightly behind you. Start with bent knees and feet off floor.

b. Lean back, and extend legs (not all the way) for one count. Return to start. Do 12 reps.

b.

Works all the ABDOMINALS!

18 dead bug

a. Lie down holding a 3-lb. weight in each hand. Start with left arm overhead and left knee lifted.

b. Take 5 seconds to lower left limb as you lift right arm and right leg. Repeat on other side. Do for 1 minute.

a.

b.

Your best total-core move!

19

see results faster

Crunches will tone the ab muscles, but cardio can help get rid of the fat layer that lies on top of the muscles. But you don't have to go crazy—just 30 minutes 3 times a week of vigorous cardio, like running, fast-walking, or hiking should do the trick.

#20

stop checking the clock

When a workout's feeling hard, you want to know when it's going to be over, but focusing on the time every few seconds will just make it feel longer. To avoid obsessing, try covering your clock or the timer on the exercise machine with a towel, or taking off your watch, so you're not tempted to peek.

work your arms!

Look great in tanks, camis and strapless tops with these moves by celeb trainer **Radu Teodorescu!**

For each of these moves, **do 4 sets of 20 reps each.** To see results fast, do these moves **3 to 4 days a week**, plus 30 minutes of cardio.

Grab a medium resistence band, two 3-pound weights, and a chair.

a.

#21
one-arm row

a. Lunge forward with
your left leg bent and
your right leg stretched
out behind you. Hold
both weights in your
right hand, letting your
arm hang straight down.
Rest your left arm on
your bent leg
for support.

b. Lift the weights
quickly up to chest
level, right alongside
your right breast, then
slowly lower them back
down to the original
hanging position.

your elbows
should
point to the
ceiling when
you lift up!

b.

#22 back contraction

a. Lean forward, back straight and parallel to the floor, legs slightly bent about one foot apart. Hold a weight in each hand and let your arms hang down, starting with the weights touching.

b. Lift your elbows to the ceiling, pulling your shoulder blades together. Bring them back until you feel it in your upper arms and the weights are lifted on either side of you, at or above chest level. Then slowly bring your arms back down to hanging position.

a.

b.

#23 chest fly

a. Tie one end of the band to a pole or banister at chest level. Standing feet shoulder-width apart, hold the band with your right hand.

b. Pull across your chest until it reaches your other arm. Be careful not to rotate your hips or shoulders.

#24 back toner

a. Wrap the band around the pole or banister between chest and waist level. Extend arms.

b. Pull the band in and down keeping arms straight, trying not to bend elbows.

a.

Be sure to keep your knees relaxed, not locked.

b.

039

get a great butt!

You will look **booty-ful** (ha!) in those new jeans with this easy plan from Rihanna's trainer, **Cindy Percival!**

All you'll need is a pair of 3-pound weights.

To see results in as little as 3 weeks, try doing 3 sets of moves, 3 times a week, plus 30 minutes of cardio three times a week! **On days** you do the moves, warm up with 5 minutes of cardio (like walking in place to music) beforehand.

#25 wall squat

a. Stand with back, shoulders, and butt pressed against a wall. Keep feet hip-width apart.

b. Slide down until thighs are parallel to floor. Hold for 1 count, then slide up. Do 10 reps.

Shift your weight so you feel it in your heels, not your toes.

a.

b.

#26
plié squat

a. Stand with your feet wide apart (toes pointed out), and hold a weight. Bend knees until thighs are parallel to floor, keeping your knees directly over your ankles.

b. Hold for 2 to 3 seconds, then straighten legs, keeping heels flat. Squeeze thighs and butt as you come up. Do 15 reps.

#27 side lunge

a. **Stand straight** with feet hip-width apart. Keep arms down, and hold a 3-lb weight in each hand.

b. **Step to right side.** Bend your right knee and sit back until thigh is almost parallel to floor. Return to start. Do 10 to 15 per leg.

a.

b.

To really target your BUTT, sit back and lunge low.

#28
toe-touch lunge

a. Stand up straight with shoulders back. Hold weights at your sides, elbows loose.

b. Step forward with left leg. Reach arms to floor on left side; bend knee so it's over ankle. Step back. Do 10 to 15 on each leg.

a.

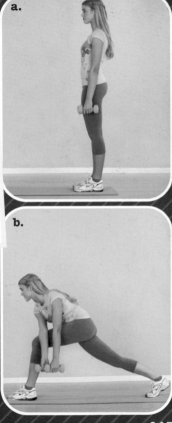

b.

sculpt your shoulders and back!

After doing these moves by celebrity trainer **Radu Teodorescu,** dresses cut low on your back will look amazing!

you'll need a set of 3-pound dumbbells

Do these moves 3 to 5 times a week, and you'll **feel stronger** in about 2 weeks!

Warm up by running in place for 1 minute, then jumping up and down for 1 minute. Circle arms forward 10 times, then backward 10 times to loosen up muscles. Then do 3 sets of each move shown, resting only 30 seconds between each set.

#29 chest press

a. Lie on your back with knees bent, feet shoulder-width apart. Rest your elbows out to the sides on the floor, holding dumbbells up to the ceiling.

b. Push the dumbbells up as you rotate your wrists inward, so your pinkies almost touch each other. Ten presses make 1 set.

a.

b.

a.

#30
chair push-up

a. Place your hands on the edge of a chair and walk your feet back until your body is straight—don't let your back arch or your butt stick out.

b. Look ahead (not down), neck aligned with spine, and keep elbows close to your sides. Slowly lower yourself as far as you can. Ten push-ups make 1 set.

b.

#31
one-arm row

a. Place right hand and right knee on the chair. Hold a weight in your left hand, letting your arm hang straight down.

b. Pull the weight straight up until your elbow points to the ceiling. Ten rows with each arm make 1 set.

a.

c.

Don't lock your elbows!

b.

#32

forward & side raise

a. Stand with your arms at your sides and feet shoulder-width apart.

b. Lift arms in front of you to eye level.

c. Immediately move arms to shoulder level and open them out to the sides. Return to position A. Moving from A to C 10 times equals 1 set.

#33 biceps curl

a. Crouch into a leapfrog position with feet slightly turned out. Hold the dumbbells with arms straight, and elbows against your inner thighs.

b. Bend both elbows to lift the dumbbells up toward your chest. Ten biceps curls make 1 set.

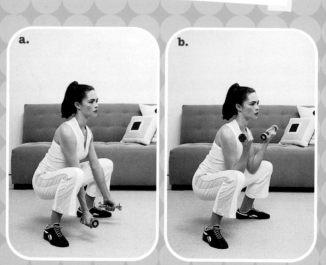

a.

b.

a.

b.

Don't lock your elbows or knees!

#34 triceps lift

a. Hold a dumbbell in each hand with your elbows shoulder-width apart and bent so that the dumbbells almost touch your back.

b. Slowly extend your arms up to the ceiling. Then bring them back down to position A. Ten times makes 1 set. Do 3 sets.

tighten your core

A strong **core** (the muscles between the shoulders and hips—basically everything that supports the spine), helps you have better posture, flatter abs, and makes it easier to do cardio. The fastest way to build one? This 10-minute workout from Pilates guru **Mari Winsor!**

For **strong, tight** abs in just 10 days, do this core-blasting workout once a day.

Keep your abs **tight** while you're doing each move.

You'll need a towel and a mat.

#35 the hundred

Put a folded towel between your knees, and lift legs 45 degrees off the floor. Raise head and pulse arms up and down by hips. Inhale as you do 5 arm pulses (up and down equals 1 pulse), then exhale as you do 5. Repeat 8 times.

#36 modified roll-up

a. Sit with knees bent and hands behind them for support. Round upper back; lean back 45 degrees.

b. Contract your abs to sit upright—but don't use your arms to help. Return to A; repeat 4 times.

#37
flutter kick

Lie flat on your back
with your hands under
your hips and feet
just off the floor. Use
lower legs to lightly
kick 50 times total.

#38 arm lift

a. Sit with knees bent and toes pointed on ground. Lean back 45 degrees and lift arms straight up.

b. Exhale and slowly lower your arms to knee level. Inhale and return to A; repeat 5 times.

#39 leg lift

a. Lie flat on your back keeping both knees bent. Lift left leg 90 degrees and lift right foot up 2 inches.

b. Lift right leg up to 90 degrees as you lower left foot to 2 inches off floor. Return to A; repeat 10 times.

#40 twisting crunch

a. With hands lightly touching your head and legs 6 inches off the floor, bring left elbow to right knee. Keep left leg straight.

b. Move right elbow to left knee; keep right leg straight. Do A and B 20 times total; hold for 2 seconds each time.

get event-ready in 2 weeks!

When stars like Jessica Alba need to get red-carpet-ready in a hurry, they call celeb trainer **Ramona Braganza**. Use her plan to transform your body in 14 days flat!

You'll need a set of 5-pound weights for this workout.

To see results fast, do 3 sets of these moves, with bursts of 5 minutes of cardio in between with little resting in between sets, 3 times a week. Do 1 day of 40 minutes of cardio each week as well.

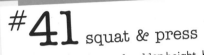

#41 squat & press

a. Holding weights at shoulder height, bend your knees and sit down into a squat.

b. Stand up and press arms overhead, keeping the weights close together. Do 20 reps.

a.

Do this for killer LEGS, BUTT and SHOULDERS.

b.

a. This moves shapes up your THIGHS and BUTT.

b.

#42 ballet squats

a. Stand with feet wide and knees out. Bend knees; keep your back straight.

b. Contract butt muscles as you rise and return to start position. Do 15 reps.

#43

leg & biceps curl

a. Place right foot on chair. Balance on left foot. Hold weights at your side.

b. Curl arms, palms up, and at the same time bend your left knee (don't let it go over your toe). Do 10 reps per side.

This tightens your BUTT, LEGS, and ARMS.

#44

seated triceps dip

a. Hold on to edge of seat, with arms straight and knuckles facing forward.

b. Lower butt toward floor until arms are at a 90-degree angle. Do 20 reps.

a.

b.

This strengthens your ABS, ARMS, LEGS, BUTT and BACK!

#45

arm & leg burn

a. Balance on right leg, holding your body parallel to floor and a weight in your left hand, hanging down to the floor.

b. Bring your elbow back toward the ceiling, pulling the weight towards your ribs. Keep your left foot flexed. Do 10 reps per side.

#46 push-up & plank

a. Get into the push-up position with your back straight. Do 10 push-ups.

b. Afterward, hold plank position (top position of the push-up) for 30 seconds, stomach tight.

a.

b.

get a better body in one move!

Get toned exactly where you want with these moves from Ashley Tisdale's trainer, **Candice Richardson.** Each one works super-fast on the body part you want to show off!

These exercises target **multiple** muscles at once, so you get a total-body workout in less moves. Do the series of moves 3 times a week and you'll start to see results in **1 month**!

Some moves require **more than 1 set**, so pause in-between for 30 seconds.

You'll need any hardcover book and 3-pound weights.

a.

b.

#47 lunge jump

a. Step into lunge position: Keep front foot flat, back foot on its toes, and legs at 90-degree angles.

b. Push off front foot and jump straight up, landing with legs together. Lunge with other leg; repeat. Do 2 sets of 12 reps.

a. For even better results, lift your shoulders off the floor and look at your THIGHS the whole time!

#48 single leg drop

a. Lie on your back with your arms resting at your sides and both legs in the air forming a "tabletop" (Keep your knees together and directly above your hips.)

b. Slowly straighten 1 leg, extending and lowering it to about 2 inches off the floor. Slowly return to start and repeat with your other leg. That's 1 rep: Do 3 sets of 15.

b.

#49 backside rocker

a. With your heels elevated on a book, crouch down and grab the back of your ankles.

b. Keep hands on ankles as you straighten legs and raise butt in air. Quickly return to start. Do 3 sets of 20.

a.

Your chest should be touching your THIGHS.

b.

Keep your arms at 90-degree angles, as if you were holding trays.

#50 serving trays

a. Hold weights at waist level with palms up and fists pointing out to each side.

b. Bring weights together in front of you; return to start. Do 3 sets of 15.

#51 twist press

a. Hold dumbbells at chin level, just outside your shoulders, with palms facing in.

b. Straighten arms overhead as you twist to the left. Return to start. Repeat to right side. Do 3 sets of 12.

a.

b.

Be sure to stay put as you twist at the WAIST!

#52

keep it slow and steady

When you're doing moves with multiple sets, it's easy to forget good form by the end. Instead of rushing through, make sure to pause between each set, checking that your spine is straight, head lifted, butt tucked in, and shoulders back. This helps you breathe easier and avoid straining your arms, back and neck.

#53

count down

When you can't resist looking at the clock, try to set the timer or your watch so it's counting down, instead of counting up. So instead of seeing that you've completed 10, 15, or 20 minutes, change the setting so that it shows how much time you have left to make you feel like you're "running out of time."

fat-burning workout

Get your heart pumping with this fat-blasting cardio routine by celeb fitness trainer **Radu Teodorescu**.

You'll need running shoes and a stopwatch or a wristwatch with a second hand

Go from one move to the next **without** stopping, and repeat the entire series 3 times, resting only **30 seconds** between each set of moves. Work up to doing each move for 1 minute. Do the whole thing 3 times a week for fast results.

Start by warming up: **Shake out** your arms and legs for 10 counts each. Then jog in place for about 2 minutes before starting **Move 1**.

#54
knees-up

Briskly run in place, bringing your knees up and as close to your chest as possible, for 20 seconds.

a.

#55
forward dips

a. Slow down and run lightly in place for 3 counts.

b. Step three feet in front of you with your left foot, lifting your right foot behind you and reaching your right hand down about 6 inches off the floor. Bounce back up then step forward with your right foot. Do this for 20 seconds, alternating sides.

b.

#56

heels-up run

Briskly run in place, kicking your heels as close to your butt as possible, for 20 seconds. Repeat 8 times.

#57 diagonal dips

a. Slow down and run lightly in place for 5 counts.

b. Step 3 feet to your left with your left foot, bringing your right foot up behind you and reaching your right hand down to about 6 inches off the floor. Bounce back up, then step to the right with your right foot. Do this for 20 seconds, continuing to alternate feet.

a.

b.

#58
front lifts

Run in place as you lift your legs straight out in front of you as high as you can. Do this for 20 seconds.

#59
high jumps

Jump straight up and
down for 20 seconds,
keeping your hands
on your hips.

#60
back lifts

Run in place, lifting your legs behind you as high as you can. Do this for 20 seconds.

#61
cool down & stretch

Cross your right leg over your left knee, and pull your left leg as close to your chest as you can. You'll feel the stretch in your butt, lower back, and hamstrings. Hold for 10 counts, switch legs, and repeat.

That's Radu!

#62 it's in the breathing

You'll know you're working hard enough when your breathing gets heavier, and having a conversation is a little difficult.

get bikini-ready in 4 weeks!

Feel your hottest in that new suit with these moves from **Gregory Joujon-Roche**—he's trained the ultimate beach babe, Gisele Bündchen.

Week one: Do the moves and 20 minutes of cardio twice.

Week two: Same thing, plus try to spot exercise opportunities in your daily life, like taking the stairs at the mall instead of the escalator.

You'll need two 3-pound weights.

Week three: Do the moves plus 20 minutes of cardio 3 times this week. Double the time you hold the Superwoman and the Bridge.

Week four: Do the moves 4 times, plus cardio 3 times (on separate days or together).

#63

arms: outside biceps curl

a. Sitting or kneeling with back straight, hold a weight in each hand. Let elbows touch waist.

b. Inhale for 2 counts as you lift the weights, palms up; exhale for 5 counts as you lower them. Do 3 sets of 20.

a.

b.

Try to land lightly, like a cat, so you won't hurt your knees.

#64

legs: rocket jump squat

a. Stand with feet wide apart, and lower into a squat. Then leap into the air, keeping abs tight.

b. Land with your feet together and slowly bend your knees. Jump back to position A landing with legs together. Do 3 sets of 15.

#65 chest: total push-up

a. Get into an upside-down V pose. Keeping legs straight and head tucked, push back toward heels.

b. Bend elbows (like in a push-up). Swoop headfirst, as if crawling under a fence. Do 3 sets of 5.

a.

Your upper body and belly should almost scrape the ground.

b.

a.

#66 back: superwoman

a. Lie on your stomach with your arms out in front of you and head facing forward. As you lower yourself, squeeze your butt and arms.

b. Lift everything but your belly off the floor. Hold for at least 30 seconds. Do 3 times.

b.

a.

#67 butt: bridge

a. Inhale as you lay with your feet hip-width apart, knees bent, feet flat, and arms at your side.

b. Raise hips and exhale. Lace fingers under hips; squeeze your butt. Hold for 1 to 2 minutes.

b.

#68 waist: accordion crunch

a. Lie on your back, with head up and elbows pointed out. Bend your knees and flex your feet. Don't interlace your fingers—stay relaxed when pulling yourself up. Make your abs do all the work.

b. Inhale as you touch your knees to your elbows. Exhale on the way down. Do 3 sets of 15.

a.

b.

Do **1 set of 4 reps** on each side at least twice a week. Hold each stretch for 15 to 20 seconds.

increase your flexibility!

Here's a flexibility routine from celeb fitness guru **Radu Teodorescu** to add to the cardio and strength-training workouts you already do for a long and lean body.

You'll need: a set of 3-pound weights and a mat or a carpeted room.

#69 push over

a. Reach your right arm in front and slightly to your left. Brace your right elbow with the back of your left hand.

b. Use your left arm to push your right arm toward your left shoulder as far as you can, keeping your right arm straight and palm facing you. Hold the stretch. Switch arms, alternating until you do a full set on both sides.

a.

b.

a.

#70 arm twister

a. Stand with your feet shoulder-width apart. Interlace your fingers in front of your chest, with elbows out and palms facing you.

b. Keeping fingers laced, turn your palms outward and straighten your elbows. Twist your upper body to the left. Hold the stretch. Return to center and alternate sides for a total of 4 reps on each side.

#71 leaning tower

a. Stand with feet shoulder-width apart. With both arms overhead, clasp your right wrist with your left hand.

b. Looking slightly up and to your left, lean over as far as you can while pulling your right wrist into a deeper stretch. Hold it, then stand upright. Switch sides, then alternate for 4 reps on each side.

a.

b.

#72
modified seated hurdle

a. Sit with your left leg in front of you at a slight angle and your right foot touching your left inner thigh.

b. Lengthen your body as you lean over your left leg and gently pull your toes to get closer to your leg. Hold the stretch. Repeat on the other side, alternating for a total of 4 reps on each side.

101

#73
the pretzel

a. Sit on the floor with your left leg stretched out and to the left. Cross your right leg over your left knee.

b. Place your left elbow on your right knee and your right hand on the floor behind you. Twist to your right as you press your right knee to the left with your elbow. Hold the stretch, then alternate to do 4 reps on each side.

a.

#74
booty stretch

a. Lie on your back and bend your right leg, lifting your foot off the ground. Cross you left leg over your right knee; hold your right thigh. Elevate your head and shoulders.

b. Pull leg into your chest as you lower your head and shoulders to the floor. Hold the stretch, then alternate sides for a full set of 4 reps on each side.

b.

#75 sidebender

a. Hold a set of weights in left hand and stand with feet shoulder-width apart, right hand behind head.

b. Bend to the left until weights are at knee level. Return to center; repeat 25 times per side daily. Work up to 100 reps per side to sculpt waist in 2 weeks.

a.

b.

#76
flexibility is key!

Increased flexibility not only helps you during your workout—it also helps your muscles recover from workouts, gives you better posture, and helps with coordination.

#77
stretching for success!

let your new-found flexibility help you in all areas of your life! It is much easier to handle stress when you're willing to bend.

get spring-break ready!

Piloxing is a cool mix of Pilates and boxing designed to make you sleek like a ballerina and powerful like a boxer. Do these total-body tummy-tightening moves from Vanessa Hudgen's trainer **Vivica Jenkins** and you'll rock those shorts and tanks!

Do this series of moves just **3 times** a week—you'll tighten and tone every little body part you forgot about this winter!

Try not to pause **too long** between moves to get the full cardio benefit!

#78

power move #1: burn out

a. Stand with your feet shoulder width apart and your fists up in front of your face like a boxer. Punch straight forward with one arm.

b. Recoil that arm, then punch with the other one. Keep doing this as quickly as possible for 15 seconds, then rest. Repeat 2 more times.

a.

b.

The faster you go, the better the cardio-it'll slim you down!

a.

Balancing is hard but worth it—your muscles work twice as hard!

b.

#79

sleek move #1: serve the platter

a. Stand on your left leg with your knee bent. Your right leg is lifted in a bent position in front of you, and your arms are bent and palms are up like you're holding a tray close to your body.

b. Pretend you're serving the platter by straightening your arms and right leg out in front of you. Return to start. Do 3 sets of 8 reps on each leg.

109

a.

b. Get low! You should feel a little burn in your BUTT and LEGS.

#80

power move #2: drive the car

a. Stand with feet shoulder-width apart and your knees bent. Reach your arms straight out in front of your chest, like you're grabbing a steering wheel.

b. Steer the car to the right and then to the left. Make big turns and really bend at your sides until you feel a squeeze. Do this for 15 seconds, then rest. Repeat 2 more times.

a. Even though you're tilted back, your spine is in a straight line!

#81

sleek move #2: spinal twist sit-up

a. Sit on the floor with your legs bent in front of you. Lift your arms up in the air and lean back slightly.

b. Pull one bent knee into your chest as you twist your body and touch the opposite elbow to that knee. Return to the center, twist to the other side and repeat. That's a rep. Do 3 sets of 8 reps.

b.

#82

power move #3: criss cross

a. Stand with your feet shoulder-width apart and your knees bent. Keep your fists close to your face.

b. Jump up and land with your right foot crossed in front of the left one, as shown. Jump back to the starting position, then jump again and land with the left foot in front. Do for 15 seconds, then rest. Repeat 2 more times.

a.

b.

The key is staying light on your feet when you land. Don't Stomp!

a.

Really pretend like you're pushing against something heavy. It'll tone your shoulders faster!

b.

#83
sleek move #3: raise the roof

a. Stand with feet together and knees bent, placing all of your weight on your right leg. Put your hands by your ears with palms up and elbows bent.

b. Extend your left leg out to the side and tap your toe on the floor while straightening your arms to the ceiling. (Just pretend you're "raising the roof!") Return to start. Do 3 sets of 8 on each leg.

get a total-body workout!

Look lean and toned all over with easy routine that works every muscle group from celeb trainer **Radu Teodorescu.**

Do **3 to 5** sets of each move, 3 to 4 times a week, to see a noticeable difference in 4 weeks. Go by how your body feels, making sure to **pause** in between so your body has a chance to rest

You'll need two 3-pound weights (or two 1-liter water bottles).

a.

#84 arms: push-up with a kick

a. Get into a push-up position with straight arms and legs. Keep your neck straight and in line with your spine.

b. Bend your arms slightly and slowly kick your right leg up behind you. Return to position A. Work your way up to five reps on each side, doing three to five sets for each leg.

b.

a.

b.

c.

Work your way up to completing 10 circles and up to five sets

#85 arms: weight circles

a. Standing with feet shoulder-width apart, grab one 3-lb dumbbell in each hand, and extend your arms into a Y formation above your head.

b. Rotate your arms in a circle by bringing them behind you. Keep your elbows and back straight.

c. Moving your arms so they come down to your sides, then bring them back into a Y.

#86 legs: squat jump

a. With your legs shoulder-width apart, bend your knees and lean slightly forward.

b. Push off, straighten your legs, and swing your arms upward. Repeat 10 times for one set.

a.

b.

Reach to the sky to really work your whole body!

a.

b.

Take small hops!

#87 legs: one-legged hop

a. Stand on your left leg with your knee slightly bent. Hold your right leg behind you with your right hand.

b. Hop on your left leg 10 times, then switch sides and repeat on your right leg for 1 set.

Use your abs to crunch up!

#88 abs: v and tuck

a. Sit on your tailbone with your arms out to the sides and legs up at a 45-degree angle.

b. Grab your right knee and pull it toward your chest. Go back to position A and repeat on the left. Work your way up to 10 tucks on each side for 1 set.

#89 abs: jackknife

a. Lie back with your left knee bent and your left arm above your head.

b. Sit up while raising your right leg and reaching your left arm to meet it. Then lower yourself back to position A. Work your way up to 10 reps on each side for 1 set.

Kick as high as you can!

your weekend workout!

When you think of exercise, the word "fun" doesn't always come to mind. But with this easy routine from Emma Roberts's trainer, **Kathy Kaehler**, you won't feel like you're working out!

You'll need a Hula Hoop, a deck of cards, your MP3 player, and a jump rope.

You don't always have time to exercise during the week, so make the most of Saturday and Sunday—just **6** moves to do each day.

#90 hula!

It's great for the waist. Aim for 4 minutes.

a.

#91
balance!

a. Stand on one leg and lift the other back behind you. Put arms straight out to the side.

b. Lean forward with back flat and lift your leg up as high as you can. Hold for count of 30 and then bring it down. Repeat with other leg.

b.

Balancing really works your CORE!

#92 count cards!

a. Stand with your feet hip-width apart, weight on your heels. Hold 20 cards in your hands.

b. Squat and drop a card; return to A. Repeat until you've dropped and picked up all the cards one by one.

a.

b.

Really works your BUTT and THIGHS!

#93
jump rope!

Try to jump 100 times without messing up, or for 2 minutes straight!

a.

Do this move 3 times total!

b.

#94 bridge back bend

a. Sit with knees bent and hands behind you, fingers facing forward.

b. Use arms and legs to lift butt so back is straight. Hold for 10 seconds.

#95

dance!

Set your MP3 player on a shake-your-booty song and dance until it's over.

get a dancer's body

Look longer and leaner—and improve your coordination—with this routine by Radu Teodorescu.

Do the series of moves 3 times a week, and you'll see results in **3 weeks**. Since each move requires multiple sets, rest for 30 seconds between each set.

You'll need a ballet bar or kitchen counter to hold for support and comfortable clothes you can stretch in.

#96 calf raise: balance & leg stretch

a. Stand with your heels together, feet turned out as shown, arms softly bent in front of you.

b. Lift heels as high off the ground as you can, raising your arms over head. Hold for 1 count. Return to position A. Ten raises makes 1 set. Do 3 to 5 sets.

a.

b.

a.

b.

#97
lunge lift: hips & thighs

a. Hold bar or counter with your left hand for balance. Get into the lunge position shown, with both feet turned slightly out. Hold your right arm out in front of you.

b. Raise your right arm overhead and swing your right leg out in front of you as high as you can. Return to position A. Ten lifts on each leg (20 lifts total) makes 1 set. Do 3 to 5 sets.

#98
arabesque lift: butt & lower back

a. Hold on to the bar or counter, lift your right foot a few inches off the ground and point your foot, turning it out to the right. Hold your right arm straight out.

b. Keeping your back straight and your right leg turned out so that your kneecap faces the wall to your right, swing your right leg behind you. Return to position A. Ten lifts with each leg is a set. Do 3 sets.

a.

b.

a.

b.

#99
side lift: thighs & shoulders

a. Holding onto the bar or counter with your left hand, stand with feet turned out, right foot in front of left, as shown. Hold your right arm over your head, softly bent.

b. Raise right leg straight out to the side as you lower your right arm. (Be sure to keep your back straight, and don't bend at the waist.) Return to position A. Ten lifts on each leg is 1 set. Do 3 sets.

135

#100
side step: rhythm & coordination

a. Start with your feet turned out, left foot in front of the right, as shown. Slightly bend your arms in front of you.

b. With your left foot, hop about 2 feet to the left as you extend your arms diagonally. When you land, your right leg should be pointed. Hold for 1 count and return to position A. 10 hops on each side is a set. Do 3 sets.

a.

b.

you'll feel the stretch in your ABS, LEGS, and ARMS.

#101
body wave: posture & coordination

a. Stand with feet together, knees slightly bent, arms out in front of your body.

b. Swing arms back in a smooth motion, like a backward circle. As arms go back, push your hips forward.

c. Continue the circle, until your arms are in a wide V. Repeat 10 times.

total body work-out in 17 minutes!

Are you too busy to tone up? Not anymore! Do these quick moves from celebrity trainer **Keli Roberts** for a hotter body in just a few weeks!

Do these **6 moves** 3 times a week to see results in under a month!

Some moves need more than one set, so pause for 30 seconds in between.

Start by dancing to your favorite song for 3 minutes—it will get you pumped up to exercise!

you'll need a soccer ball or a basketball.

#102 squat swing

a. With your feet far apart and your back flat, swing the ball between your legs.

b. Push your hips forward to bring your body and your arms up. Do 2 sets of 10.

a.

One minute to sleeker LEGS!

b.

a.

Two
minutes
to
sculpted
THIGHS!

b.

#103 side bounce

a. Stand with your feet shoulder-width apart and your toes pointed out at an angle.

b. Cross your right foot behind your left. Bounce the ball to the left. Perform 8 on each side.

a.

104
lunge bounce

a. Stand with your legs shoulder-width apart and your toes facing forward.

b. Step out to the right, lean down, and bounce the ball. Switch sides; do 10 on each side.

b.

Two minutes to a better BUTT!

#105 ball crunch

a. Lie back with your hands behind your head and the ball between your knees.

b. Squeeze the ball with your knees as you lift your shoulders off the floor. Do 2 sets of 8.

a.

Three minutes to a flatter TUMMY!

b.

a.

Three minutes to toned ABS!

#106 jump thrust

a. Squat with your feet together, holding the ball on the floor in front of you.

b. Jump your feet into plank position (your hands and feet on the ground, your back straight), then jump back to position A. Do 2 sets of 4.

b.

144

a.

b.

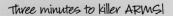

Three minutes to killer ARMS!

107 push-up

a. Get into a push up position, with your right hand resting on the ball.

b. Keep your abs tight as you bend your arms for the push-up. Do 8 on each arm.

get sexy abs, arms, & legs!

Perfect for Prom season, celeb trainer **Radu Teodorescu's** work-out will have you looking tight, toned and dress-ready fast! Do it with a friend, and you'll both look killer!

Do this workout **3 times** per week and your abs, arms and legs will look amazing in just 1 month.

Some moves require more than 1 set, so pause for **30 seconds** before beginning your next set.

#108 arms:
upper-body strengthener

a. Step toward your partner so that your front legs are 12 inches apart. Bend your elbows 90 degrees. After she touches her palms together, place your wrists outside hers.

b. Then, resist while she pushes her hands apart until they're just beyond her shoulders. In one continuous motion, return to A. Do 3 sets of 25, then switch.

#109 arms: triceps press

a. Face your partner with your feet shoulder-width apart. Bend your arms so your hands are at shoulder level and place your hands (palms down) over hers (palms up).

b. While your partner resists, press your hands down to waist level. Return to position A in one motion. Do 3 sets of 25, then switch.

#110

legs: backward leg extension

a. Face your partner and join right hands. Crouch down and lean away from each other for balance.

b. Stand up on left leg while swinging right leg back and left arm out to the side. Return to A, switch arms, and repeat on other leg. Do 3 sets of 10 on each side.

111

legs: modified bicycle

a. Lie back, lean on your elbows, and press the soles of your feet against your partner's. You both will extend your right legs while bending your left legs.

b. Switch by extending your left leg and resisting with your right. Repeat 10 times on each leg.

a.

b.

#112
legs: quads press

a. Lie on your back with your knees slightly bent. Have your partner lean into you so her chest is resting on your feet and her hands are resting behind your upper thighs.

b. While she balances on the balls of her feet, bend your legs into your chest. Return to A. Do 10 times, then switch with your partner.

a.

b.

113

abs: lower abdominal flexion

a. Lie on your back as your partner stands behind you. Grab her legs just below the knees and lift your legs until she can touch your toes.

b. Have your partner push your legs away. As she does, tighten your abs to help stop your feet from hitting the ground. Go back to A. Repeat 10 times. Switch.

#114

abs: patty-cake sit-up

a. While you and your partner lie on your backs, alternate your legs so that your right ankles are stabilized between each other's legs.

b. Pull yourself to a sitting position using your abs, and touch right hands. Return to A. Sit up again—this time touching left hands. Repeat 10 times with both hands.

a.

b.

115
listen to your body

When working out with a friend, it can be tempting to try to outdo each other in reps or sets. Competition can motivate you, but don't push yourself too hard. If you start to feel exhausted, your muscles are burning, or you feel sharp, shooting pain, stop!

116 go with the flow

When you've got the moves down, getting lost in your own head will help you focus on the moment not when the workout will end. Try listening to lyrics of a song, interpreting them in different ways, relating them to your life, or your your friend's lives. Eventually, your train of thought will help you pass the time.

the no-excuses workout!

No time, no gym membership, no idea where to start? **No problem!** If you can set aside just 1 hour total this week (20 minutes on 3 days) you'll be on your way to a hotter, happier, healthier you!

You can do this anywhere: your bedroom, your living room, the park, and all you need is you!

1. Do **1 set** of each of these exercises with minimal rest between moves. That's called a **circuit,** and doing it quickly will keep your heart rate up and sneak some **cardio** in as you tone your muscles!

2. Rest for a minute or 2, and then **repeat** the whole circuit. Your goal is to be able to do it 3 times!

#117 step-out lunge

a. Stand with your feet about shoulder-width apart and your hands on your hips.

b. Step forward with your right leg, keeping your back leg straight. Go as far as you can—but make sure that your right knee doesn't go past your toe—or until you feel a stretch. Return to start. Do 10 reps on each leg.

a.

b.

a.

b.

#118 side-step squat

a. Stand so that your feet are about shoulder-width apart, placing each hand at the side of your hips.

b. Step to the left so that your foot points out at a 45-degree angle, keeping your knee behind your toe. Your right leg stays straight and to the side. Bend at the waist, driving your hips back and keeping your back flat. Return to start. Do 10 reps to each side.

Defines your ABS, ARMS, and LEGS!

a.

#119
bridge in-and-outs

a. Start in a bridge: It's a push-up position except that your forearms are under your chest and make an upside down "V" shape to hold you up. Then lift your right leg up off the ground as far as you can, keeping it straight.

b. Bring that right leg out to the side, then bring it back in to the middle. Do 12 reps with each leg.

b.

a.

Shapes
your LEGS
and
BUTT!

b.

#120
high-knee squats

a. Stand with feet at least shoulder-width apart and hands by your face, like a boxer. Squat down, driving your hips back and leaning forward slightly.

b. Come up from the squat, bringing your right knee up to your chest as you push your arms down next to your knee. Return to squat and repeat, this time raising your left leg. That's a rep. Do 12 reps total.

a.

To get the most out of this move, don't rest when switching legs; go right from one to the other!

#121 reverse push-ups

a. Sit on your butt with your legs straight out in front of you and your feet together. Your hands are behind you with your fingers facing forward.

b. Lift your body up, pushing off your heels and keeping your legs straight and abs tight. Raise your left leg about 6 inches off the ground and lower it without touching the ground. Do 10 reps and then repeat on the other side.

b.

122
de-stress!

Justin ends every workout by walking all of his clients through a 2 to 3 minute mini-meditation. It's all about deep breathing, de-stressing, loving your body, remembering how good you feel after the workout and visualizing what the exercise is going to do for you and your body in the future.

123 give it five

To get yourself to get out there, just tell yourself to do five minutes. If you feel like stopping after that, you can quit. Most likely, once you start, you'll feel so great you won't want to stop.

dance your way to a better body!

Whether you want to look great at a club or just have fun getting fit, this routine from celebrity choreographer **Jamie King** will make your body rock!

Do this workout **once through** 3 times a week to burn fat, and keep your core strong and lean.

a.

b.

You'll feel this in your ABS, SHOULDERS, and BACK.

#124 knee lift

a. Stand with your right leg forward and slightly bent and your left leg back and straight. Angle your body towards the left side. Flex left arm by holding it straight out in front of you, then bending your forearm and squeezing your fist. Put your right hand on your hip.

b. Lift right knee as you pull left elbow down towards it. Do 16 reps on each side.

125 side step

a. Step out to the side with left foot and extend arms straight out to both sides at shoulder level. Your palms should be facing down.

b. Bring left foot in; cross arms in front of you. Do 8 reps on each side.

a.

b.

This works out your UPPER BACK and CHEST.

#126 arm pump

a. Raise right arm straight above your head, stepping forward with left heel. Your toes should be lifted off the ground.

b. Step your feet back together and bend your arm backwards behind your right shoulder. Do 32 reps per arm.

a.

b.

This move targets your TRICEPS. Alternate your feet every time you pump your arm.

a.

b.

Lunges tighten your HAM-STRINGS and QUADS.

127 deep lunge

a. With your arms raised to shoulder level, step into a lunge with your left leg. Keep your back straight and your abs tucked in.

b. Lower your right knee to floor, without allowing your left knee to go past your toes, and pull yourself up. (Don't push with hands!) Do 4 reps per side.

look hot for back-to-school!

Do celeb trainer Radu Teodorescu's workout, whenever you need to feel good fast! The trick is to build in sets of cardio and strength-training all-in-one workout (the cardio burns fat, and the strength moves define muscles).

You'll need 3-pound weights for all the moves.

Do **both** cardio and strength-training moves 2 times through, resting for only **30 seconds** between sets, 4 times a week and be toned by Labor Day!

cardio set 1

#128
run for 30 seconds, as fast as you can.

a. Lift your knees as high as you can as you run in place. Pump your arms.

#129
lunge for 30 seconds.

b. Lunge, reach right, then stand. Lunge, reach left, then stand. Repeat.

c.

130

twist for 30 seconds.

c. Hop and twist from left to right; swivel arms at chest, away from legs. Rest for 30 seconds, then move to Cardio Set 2!

cardio set 2

#131
run for 30 seconds.

a. Kick your heels up toward your butt as you run in place.

#132
skate for 30 seconds.

b. Cross left leg in front of right. Stand; do on other leg. Repeat.

c.

#133
hop for 30 seconds.

c. Hop to the right; push hips **far right** as you swivel arms left. Switch sides.

Pull your butt forward as you lunge so that you feel a stretch in your back.

#134
front lunge

a. Stand with your feet together. Hold weights at shoulder level.

b. Lunge forward on right leg; lift arms. Repeat with your left leg. Repeat 10 times.

135 side lunge

a. Feet shoulder-width apart, lunge sideways to the right reaching your left arm to your right foot.

b. Stand up, pulling weight across chest and up. Do 10; repeat with the other side.

a.

keep your back flat.

b.

a.

b.

#136 bent row

a. Squat, feet shoulder-width apart, back parallel to ground. Twist left, with left elbow up, reaching right arm to ground. Stick butt out.

b. With back still flat, twist right, reaching left arm to ground. Return to position A. Do 10 on each side.

a.

Keep your toes pointed.

b.

#137
leg pull

a. Lie on your back with legs straight up and arms overhead by your ears.

b. Open legs and do a crunch, bringing arms toward center, until your chest is up off the ground. Repeat. Do 10 reps.

a.

b.

#138
cross punch

a. Sit in a V pose, butt on the ground, so your abs are holding up your upper body. Extend right leg, and reach left arm toward your right foot. Hold abs tight, trying not to touch the floor for support.

b. Switch legs, bringing right arm toward left foot. Do 20 reps total (10 on each side).

139
take it outside

To make your body work even harder, do these moves in the sand at the beach!

140
pat yourself on the back

Think about how accomplished you'll feel when you're finished. No matter what mood you're in when you start working out, you will always leave feeling proud of yourself. When you feel like quitting, think about all the good feelings you know will come right after you're done.

countdown to new year's workout!

Motivating yourself to exercise in winter isn't easy, so this is what you need—a fun plan that gives you results **fast!**

Don't count reps. Just do each move as many times as you can in 60 seconds. Repeat the whole cycle 3 times on 3 days **each week.**

Before each strength cycle, get your heart rate up for 5 minutes. Here are some ideas— to make it really fun, do **1 minute** of each:

* Run up and down the **stairs.**
* Do jumping jacks.
* Shadowbox with yourself.
* Do **karate** kicks.
* Dance to music.

Firm up your THIGHS and BUTT!

#141

plié with heel raise

a. Stand with toes turned out and 3 feet between your heels. Lower into a deep plié squat.

b. Keeping your abs sucked in and chest lifted; rise up onto your toes. Return to squat. Hold this position for a few seconds to tone your inner thighs.

a.

To really work your ABS, put your hands behind your head!

b.

#142
lunge with kick

a. Step forward with right foot. Lower into a lunge until both knees are bent at a right angle.

b. Kick left leg up and forward until you're standing, then swing leg back into lunge. Do 30 seconds on each side.

185

Shape your
ARMS!

#143 crab push-up

a. Sit with knees bent and hands behind you, fingers facing heels. Lift your butt slightly off the ground.

b. Raise your butt until shoulders, hips, and knees are in a line. Lower back down to start. If you feel this in your legs, shift your weight back onto your arms.

a. Before starting, be sure you have lots of room to move forward.

#144
caterpillar

a. Stand with body folded at waist and hands on ground in front of feet. You can bend knees slightly.

b. Walk hands out until you're in a push-up position. Then walk feet in until you're back to the starting position.

b.

a.

145 superpower plank

a. Get on your knees in a modified push-up position (arms under shoulders and feet off the floor).

b. Lower onto your forearms one arm at a time, then come back up to start one arm at a time.

b.

Keep your ABS and BUTT tight to make this move even more effective.

146
don't give up, bundle up

It can be hard to stick to your workout when the weather gets colder—who wants to get up early when it's freezing out, or work out when it's already dark? Remember, there is no bad weather, just the wrong clothes! Make sure you've got plenty of warm layers to pile on so you'll be warm and dry on your way to and from working out!

147 get the right gear

When you know you look good, you want to show it off, so before starting a new workout, why not buy yourself a cute workout outfit for a little extra motivation to get out there?

189

boost your energy!

Get your heart pumping with these totally fun—and totally easy—aerobic moves. They work better than caffeine!

Do this circuit once through 3 times a week to rev up and get a burst of energy any time you need it.

Challenge Yourself: Start with 15-second sets, then work your way up to 30-second sets.

Warm up. Circle your arms forward 10 times, and then circle them backward 10 times.

Bend down to touch your toes while standing up. Come back up and stretch arms straight over your head. Do 10 reps.

#148 side-to-side jog

a. Stand with your feet shoulder-width apart, slightly bending your knee. Keep your arms at your sides with your elbows bent about 90 degrees. Jump as you kick your left leg out to the side.

b. As you bring down your left leg kick your right leg out to the side. Alternate sides quickly for 15 seconds to complete a set. Do 3 sets, resting for 15 seconds between sets.

a.

b.

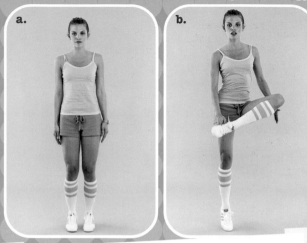

a.

b.

#149
invigorating foot tap

a. Stand with your feet slightly apart. Keep your arms down at your sides.

b. Jump and raise your left heel to thigh level (bend knee out to the side) and tap it with your right hand. As you lower your leg, start the move with your right leg. Alternate quickly for 15 seconds to complete a set. Do 3 sets, resting only briefly.

#150 balancing hop

a. Stand on your right leg. Bend your left leg and hold your foot with your left hand. Stretch your right arm forward at shoulder level.

b. Jump in place for 15 seconds. Switch legs; hop on your left foot. Hopping for 15 seconds on each leg equals a set. Do 3 sets, pausing briefly between sets. If you need to, hold out your arms for balance.

a.

b.

a.

b.

#151 high leg kick & clap

a. Stand up straight with your feet together. Keep your arms down at your sides. Keep your abs tight.

b. Jump as you kick your right leg up as high as you can. At the same time, clap your hands together under your right thigh. As you land on your right foot, kick your left leg up and repeat the move. Alternate sides quickly for 15 seconds to complete a set. Do 3 sets, with a quick rest between sets.

#152 full-body builder

a. Stand with your feet shoulder-width apart, arms down at your sides. Jump up as high as you can, while stretching your arms toward the ceiling.

b. When you land, squat down to the ground so your weight is on the balls of your feet; place hands in front of you.

a.

b.

c.

If you feel strong add a push-up!

c. **Jump** both legs back so you're in a full push-up position, then tuck your legs back into position B **quickly** and stand up. Repeat positions A through C for 15 seconds to complete a set. Do 3 sets, resting **briefly** between each.

get a better beach body!

Get a more toned butt and core in 3 weeks with these 6 simple moves from celeb fitness guru **Radu Teodorescu.**

You'll need: a beach towel or yoga mat, a medicine ball that weighs 9 to 12 pounds, or another medium-sized ball like a soccer ball or basketball.

Do **3 sets** of 10–15 reps per side (pausing for 30 seconds between sets) **3 times a week** to start. Work up to **5 sets** of 20 to 25 reps, 3 times a week.

#153 thigh lifts—glutes

a. Lie on your stomach, arms folded under your chin and right leg bent at the knee with the flat of your right foot facing the ceiling.

b. Lift your right thigh straight up as high as you can. Lower it to the ground. Repeat 9 more times. This is 1 set. Switch legs and repeat 10 times.

#154 side-to-side leg lifts

a. Place the ball at the bottom of the mat on your right side. Get on all fours. Extend your right leg.

b. Move your right leg to the left of the ball, with toes touching the ground. Then lift leg and place to the right of ball. Repeat 9 times for 1 set, then switch legs.

#155

body extension—glutes, back

a. Cross your left foot over your right and bend at the waist with arms hanging down to toes.

b. Stand up straight onto left foot as you lift right leg back and bring arms into an arch overhead as shown, keeping your body tall and squeezing your glutes. Return to start, cross right foot over left, and repeat on right foot. Do the entire sequence 9 more times for a full set.

#156

butt lift—glutes, legs, lower back

a. Lie on your back with right foot over your left knee and arms at sides.

b. Press left foot into the ground as you lift your butt as high as you can. Keep shoulders and arms planted. Return to ground. Repeat 9 more times. Switch legs and do 10 reps.

#157
the bridge—glutes, thighs

a. Sit on the ground with your knees bent, with the medicine ball between them.

b. Lift your butt off the ground until your torso is horizontal. Hold for 3 seconds, squeezing your knees and glutes. Don't bend your neck or drop the ball. Repeat 9 more times for a full set.

#158

"karate"
back kick

a. Step onto your right foot.
Bend your left leg, upper
body, and arms.

b. Lean onto your right leg
as you slowly kick your left
leg straight out in a
controlled motion with your
foot flexed as shown. Do 10
kicks with your left leg.
Switch legs and do 10 reps.
This is 1 set.

get strong, lean, and stress-free!

OM Yoga guru **Cyndi Lee** customized this daily routine to make you look great and feel focused so school doesn't stress you out!

For the following moves, let each one flow into the next instead of **stopping** in between, and try to **breathe deeply**—more oxygen increases energy and mental clarity.

Swing your ARMS in big circles.

159
backstroke

Stand up with your abs tucked in and your shoulders relaxed. Circle your arms backward 10 times.

Keep your HIPS straight.

#160
side bend

Touch your fingertips together over your head. Reach up and to the left for eight breaths; repeat to the right.

#161
open heart

Clasp your hands behind your back, look up, and pull your breastbone upward. Hold for eight breaths.

#162 flip it

Keeping your hands clasped, bend at the waist so your head is by your knees. Try to keep your back as straight as possible. Hold for eight breaths.

Every time you breathe in, see if you can hang a little lower!

#163 elephant

Lower your arms as far as you can and sweep slowly from side to side for eight breaths. Legs should be slightly bent, and the whole pose should feel comfortable.

Relax as you sway back and forth.

#164 spinal stretch

Sit on the ground with your left leg out and right leg bent over it. Wrap your left arm around your knee and twist to the right. Hold for eight breaths. Switch sides.

Extend your ARM and look toward it.

165 sit-up

Sit on the ground and hug your legs into your body so your feet are a few inches off the floor. Hold for 8 deep breaths.

Sit up straight to stay balanced.

Use your ABS, not your legs.

#166 roll back

Curve your back and flex your abs to rock back and forth 8 times. Repeat the sequence if you want.

work out in the park!

Tone your whole body and get some fresh air with this strength routine by celeb fitness trainer Radu Teodorescu.

For each move: Do 3 sets of 6 to 10 reps per side, 3 times a week to start. Work up to 5 sets of 10 to 15 reps, 3 times week. You'll see and feel a difference in 3 weeks.

You'll need:
a fence or rail that's about hip level, a sturdy park bench, a jungle gym or pull-up bar on a fitness trail, and a stopwatch to time the running intervals

#167

hurdle twist: waist

a. Bend your left knee and rest it on a rail or fence. Use both hands to touch your right foot.

b. Stand up and twist your torso as far to the left as you can. Quickly return to position A. Do this 6 times, then switch sides and do 6 more. This is a set.

#168
bench step-up: thighs, butt

a. Place left foot on a bench with the knee bent at a 90-degree angle. Put most of your weight on that leg.

b. Stand up on the bench while lifting your right leg out as shown. Return to position A. Do 6 times on each side for a complete set.

#169

knee tucks: lower abs

a. Hang from a jungle gym or pull-up bar with palms facing forward.

b. Using your abs, bring your knees as high into your chest as you can. Do this 6 times. This is a set.

Warning: The chin-up exercises in this section are pictured on tree branches for demonstration purposes only. Do not hang on trees and risk a branch breaking. Use a chin up bar or sturdy jungle gym instead!

#170 jumping chin-up: arms, back

a. Grab the chin-up bar with your palms facing in and hang with your knees bent, feet on the ground.

b. Push with your legs to do a chin-up. Hold your chin above the bar for 3 seconds if you can. Four chin-ups make a set.

a.

b.

#171

push-up with leg lift: chest, arms

a. Get into push-up position on the edge of a bench. Keep your back straight and butt tucked in.

b. Lower your chest toward the bench, raising your right leg as high as you can. Lower leg as you push back up. Alternate legs with each push-up. 6 push-ups make a set.

Doing short bursts of cardio (intervals) is a great way to build stamina and speed up your metabolism.

#172

running stairs: the fat burner

a. Run up stairs (or up a steep hill) for 30 seconds.

b. Stop and rest for 30 seconds. This is one set. Do 6 sets.

the targeted workout!

Get toned where you need to with this customized workout by **Steve Zim** (he helped sculpt Jessica Biel's bod!).

You'll need: a chair and a mat for floor work. A yoga mat is great, but a towel works just as well.

Find the description that matches **your body type** then do these moves plus 30 minutes of cardio 3 times a week for fast results!

#173 abs

a. Lie with knees bent, arms at sides. Crunch abs as you reach for right heel.

b. Relax, then reach for the left heel to complete 1 rep. Do 20 reps.

a.

If your TUMMY is toned-get even more defined!

b.

a.

If your TUMMY is soft-flatten it!

174 abs

a. Lie on your back with your hands placed lightly behind your neck and lift your legs into bicycle pose (your right leg bent and your left leg extended straight out). Twist and touch left elbow to right knee.

b. Switch sides, twisting right elbow to left knee, to finish the rep. Do 20 reps.

b.

a. If your BOOTY is flat-sculpt it!

b. Make sure your head and neck touch the floor to avoid strain.

#175 butt

a. Lying with arms at sides, place right foot on the seat of the chair. Cross left foot over knee.

b. Squeeze butt muscles to lift your shoulder blades off the floor. Do 20 reps, then switch legs.

#176
butt

a. Hold on to the back of the chair and lift right knee in toward chest.

b. Kick right leg straight back, holding for two counts, then lower to ground. Do 20 reps. Repeat with the left leg.

If your BOOTY is round-firm it up!.

a.

b.

#177 legs

a. Stand with feet 1 foot apart. Place hands on hips and keep shoulders back.

b. Step forward with right foot; drop left knee to the floor. Stand up. Do 20 reps per side.

a.

If your LEGS are thin–add definition!

b.

a.

#178

legs

a. Stand with hands on hips. Balance weight on left leg.

b. Tip forward until body is parallel to ground. Repeat on opposite side. Do 20 reps per side.

b.

If your LEGS are muscular—make them look long and lean!

get toned with a friend!

Friends share everything, so why not workouts? Try this 2 person workout from **Jarett Del Bene,** who's trained Lauren Conrad and Audrina Patridge, and you'll laugh the whole way through!

Exercising with a partner means built in motivation. **Plan** to meet up 3 days a week and do these moves 3 times through, resting between sets.

You'll need: 3-pound weights and any kind of ball, (a basketball works great).

a. Works your BUTT, LEGS, and ARMS!

b.

#179
lunge with weights

a. Stand up straight with your shoulders relaxed. Hold a dumbbell in each hand.

b. Step forward on one foot without letting your knee go past your toes. Return to standing position. Do 10 on each leg.

a.

#180
ball sit-ups

a. Lie on the floor, legs bent. Have your friend stand on your toes to anchor you. Toss her a ball and have her catch it.

b. Sit up as high as you can as your friend passes back the ball. Curl down and repeat 15 to 20 times.

b.

Strengthens your core for flat ABS!

235

#181
plié squat and biceps curl

a. Stand with feet wide apart and toes pointed out. Hold a dumbbell in each hand with palms out.

b. Lower yourself so your knees are bent 90 degrees. Curl the weights to your shoulders. Repeat 15 times.

Tones inner and outer THIGHS!

a.

#182 partner push-ups

a. On your hands and knees, lower your chest to the floor. (Keep head in line with spine!)

b. Come up and slap hands, alternating hands each time. Repeat 12 to 15 times.

b.

#183 hamstring curl

a. Lie on your stomach, propped up on your elbows. Have your friend put pressure on your heels.

b. Curl heels to your butt as your friend provides resistance. Do 12 to 15 reps.

#184 meet in the morning

Coordinating schedules can get tricky, so plan to meet up 3 times a week 20 minutes before school starts. Once you've worked out, you're done for the day!

#185

bra basics

If you're tempted to avoid a workout, tell yourself that all you have to do is to put on your sports bra. Once it's on, you'll be less likely put off your workout, because you've done the hard part—getting dressed!

work out with your guy!

Grab your best guy friend (or your crush) and try **Radu Teodorescu's** 2-person workout! You'll get stronger, leaner — and definitely closer!

Try this series of moves 3 times a week, plus a **20-minute** run to warm up.

You'll need: a comfy mat for the lying down moves. A comforter or doubled-up beach towel will work.

#186
lean in

a. Stand back-to-back with your knees bent and hips close but not touching. Make sure his knees and yours are bent at the same angle.

b. As he tries to run backward, resist. Run across the room; switch. Do 3 sets each way.

Pushing back tones your THIGHS and BACK!

a.

b.

c.

#187
swing on over

a. Lie head to toe on the floor, lining up your hips with his. Reach under each others' legs to hold hands.

b. Lift your legs and butt off the floor, then swing them to his other side as he swings his legs to your other side.

c. Lower your legs to the floor, then repeat in the other direction. Do 3 sets of 8.

243

a.

b.

#188
lift up

a. Sit on the ground in front of him, facing away, with your knees bent and your hands up around his neck.

b. As he supports your back, rise up to stand up, your arms arching backward. Return to the starting position. Do 3 sets of 8.

#189
seesaw

a. Facing each other, hold hands to create tension in your arms. Sit down into a low squat, as he's still standing.

b. As he lowers into a squat, straighten your legs to stand. Do 3 sets of 8.

Both partners lean back so neither falls (make sure he doesn't pull you up too hard)!

get hot in a hurry!

You're a busy girl—so Jessica Biel's trainer, **Jason Walsh,** shows you how to get strong and fit fast!

You'll need a medicine ball (you can substitute a soccer or basketball for this)

Three days a week, sandwich the moves in between 2 mini sessions of cardio, like 10 minutes of walking or running. Then do the moves in order, 3 times through. On a fourth day, play a fun sport or walk with a friend.

a.

190
single leg lift

a. Stand with your feet together and hold the ball close to your chest.

b. In one motion, bend at your waist and lift your leg so you're parallel to the floor. Return to position A and repeat 15 times on each leg.

b.

Tightens
BUTT, LEGS
& BACK!

Works LEGS & ABS!

#191 squat jumps

a. Squat with feet far apart and knees in line with toes. Hold the ball, keeping back straight.

b. Jump up, pointing toes and using your legs and butt muscles to lift up. Keep that stomach tight too! Do 15 times.

#192 core killer

Place right elbow and forearm on the floor, and rest the ball on top of your right hip. With feet straight out, lift hips toward ceiling and hold. Perform 30 seconds on each side.

Try to keep your head in line with your spine.

#193
squat & chest pass

a. Squat down and stay in that position. Hold the ball to your chest with both hands.

b. Throw the ball against a wall and catch it fast! Remain in a low squat and throw the ball 10 to 15 times.

#194
squat & rotate

a. Start with feet shoulder-width apart. Bend your knees; hold ball to the side of your left knee.

b. Slowly stand, twisting your torso to the right. Raise ball high and lift heel off the floor. Return to squat. Do 15 on each side.

a.

b.

Targets
ARMS
&
STOMACH!

a.

#195
tummy twist

a. Sit with knees bent, feet off floor. Hold ball to the left side of your body.

b. Twist torso and move ball to right side. Do 15 twists to each side.

b.

Whittles your SIDES!

253

get ready for tryouts!

Start this pre-season workout by celebrity fitness trainer **Radu Teodorescu** 3 weeks before your sports tryouts and you'll run faster, jump higher —and make the team!

Do this series of **cardio and strength intervals,** pausing only briefly between sets, 3 times a week. The quick, short bursts of activity will help you feel **stronger** and ready for the intense workouts you'll do at tryouts in just 3 weeks.

You'll need: running shoes or other good sneakers, and a long, flat area to run on, like a track or lawn.

#196

high start: speed & reaction time

a. Put most of your weight on your left leg and lean slightly forward, ready to run.

b. Start running as fast as you can. Sprint for 10 seconds. Stop and rest for 30 seconds. This is 1 interval. Do 6 intervals, switching starting legs each time.

#197
plié jump: leg strength

a. Begin in a plié position with legs about 2 feet apart, knees bent to almost 90 degrees.

b. Jump up, touching your heels together if you can. Land back in plié position. Six jumps make 1 set. Do 3 sets.

#198 spin jump: balance & coordination

a. Stand with legs more than shoulder width apart, knees slightly bent, holding arms behind you, ready to help you spin. Jump up while turning your body 180 degrees to your left.

b. You'll land facing the opposite direction. Jump again, this time spinning 180 degrees to the right. Six jumps equals 1 set. Do 3 sets.

199
power skip: coordination & leg strength

a. Take a big step forward with your left leg until you're in the lunge position shown, with most of your weight on your left leg.

b. Hop up on your left leg, bringing your right knee up as high as you can. Land in a lunge with your right leg in front. Then hop up on your right leg, bringing your left knee up. Repeat 6 to 10 times on each leg. That's 1 set; do 3 to 5 sets.

#200 kangaroo jump: jumping power

a. Stand with feet slightly apart. Bend knees and jump up as high as you can, tucking your legs into your chest.

b. Bend knees as you hit the ground to absorb the impact. Six jumps equal 1 set. Do 3 sets.

#201

track & field stretch: flexibility

a. Put your left leg out in front of you with your foot flexed. Bend the right foot to your side at about 90 degrees. Stretch toward your left foot as shown and hold for 10 counts.

b. Sit up and twist your torso as far as you can to the right, keeping your back straight and abs tight. Hold for 10 counts. Do both parts of the stretch 8 times, then switch legs and repeat.

your weekly workout!

Tone your entire body in only 25 minutes a day with this 5-day regimen from celeb trainer Harley Pasternak.

Do 2 sets of 25 reps for every move, resting 30 seconds between sets.

You'll need: a large stability ball, one small stability ball, a stool, two 3-pound weights, and an exercise mat.

MONDAY
chest, quads,
and upper abs

#202
chest press

a. With your feet about hip-width apart, lean on the larger ball, using it to support your shoulder blades and neck and keeping your legs bent. Keeping your back flat against the larger ball, hold the smaller ball right above your chest.

b. Raise the smaller ball toward the ceiling until your arms are straight in front of you. Try to keep it directly in front of your chest.

a.

b.

#203 tap squat

a. Keeping your feet about hip-width apart and your arms straight, stand just in front of the stool or chair and hold weights at your sides.

b. Squat. Lower your body carefully to the seat of the stool or chair—making sure your knees don't extend over your toes. As soon as your butt touches the stool, stand back up.

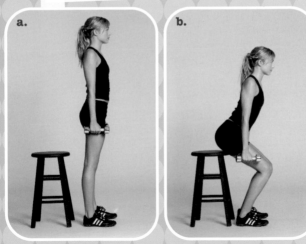

a.

b.

a.

#204 crunch

a. Lie on your back with knees bent, your feet a few inches apart, and your hands resting lightly behind your head. Stretch out your abs as much as you can.

b. Contract your abs and lift your upper back several inches off the floor, using your ab muscles to pull you up, not your hands.

a.

TUESDAY
back, hamstrings,
and sides

b.

You should feel a stretch
along the sides of
your BACK.

#205
pullover

a. With your feet about hip-width apart, lean back on the large stability ball. Keep your back flat and use the ball to support your back and shoulders. Hold one side of onedumbbell between both of your hands and lift arms up.

b. Reach your arms behind you, stopping when the weight is in line with the top of your head.

a.

b.

Keep your
BACK flat
and LEGS
straight.

#206 dead lift

a. Keeping your feet hip-width apart and
arms straight, hold weights at your
sides.

b. Slide hips back, extending your neck
and back for balance. Keep your back
flat and your head and chest lifted up.

#207 side bend

a. Keeping your feet hip-width apart, hold a weight at your side.

b. Keep your arms straight and lean to the side, making a curve at your waist and letting the weight slide along the leg you are leaning toward. Lean only your upper body to the side as far as you can, lengthen

a.

b.

Take WEDNESDAY off!

THURSDAY
chest, quads,
and lower abs

a.

#208
chest fly

a. Hold your feet in a wide stance a few feet apart. Lean on the larger medicine ball so that it supports your neck and shoulder blades. Hold weights together in both hands.

b. Pull the weights away from each other until they are spaced wider apart than your feet.

b.

Keep your ARMS slightly bent and on the same level.

a.

b.

Alternate
LEGS with
each move
forward.

#209
walking lunge

a. Keeping your feet only slightly apart and your arms straight, hold weights at your sides.

b. Step forward into a deep lunge—until your knee is only slightly above the ground—keeping your butt tucked under, and your back straight. Keep your arms straightened at your sides, and make sure your standing knee does not bend past the line of your toes.

a.

b.

#210
lower crunch

a. Lie on your back with knees bent and your feet raised several inches off the ground. Keep your arms straightened and at your sides.

b. Contracting your abs, lift your hips a few inches off the floor. Be careful to use your abs to lift you and not your arms. Keep your arms straight at your sides through the movement.

Squeeze your lower ABS as you lift.

a.

b.

Keep your
BACK parallel
to the floor.

FRIDAY
back, shoulders,
and abs

#211
dumbbell row

You can use the seat of a couch to do this move.

a. Hold one weight in your hand. Rest one knee and your free hand on the bench. Keep the other leg extended to the side. Keep the arm with the weight straight and hold it several inches away from the bench.

b. Keep your head up and pull the weight toward your ribs until the weight is parallel to the bench.

273

#212 shoulder press

a. Sit on the edge of the stool or chair, keeping your back straight and your feet slightly wider than hip-width apart. Hold weights at right angles on either side of your head.

b. Extend your arms straight as you press weights to ceiling. Lift the weights up and toward each other.

a.

b.

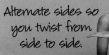

Alternate sides so you twist from side to side.

#213 ab twist

a. Keep your feet a few inches apart and your arms straightened by your sides. Contract your abs and sit halfway up with your knees partially bent.

b. Twist and reach one arm across to the opposite side of your body.

a.

b.

SATURDAY
arms and abs!

#214 biceps curl

a. Sit on the edge of the stool or chair, keeping your back straight and your feet slightly wider than hip width apart. Keeping your arms straight, hold weights by your sides.

b. Bend elbows toward your body, keeping the weights straight and horizontal (parallel to the ground).

#215 triceps press

a. Holding weights, stand with your back straight and your feet only slightly apart. Bend elbows behind your body as if you are scratching your back, so that you are holding weights behind your head.

b. Straighten arms above your head, keeping the weights straight and horizontal (parallel to the ground).

a.

b.

Keep upper ARMS parallel to your ears.

#216 double crunch

a. Lie on your back on the floor with your knees bent up and your feet together, lifted slightly off the ground. Place your hands lightly behind your neck.

b. Lift shoulders and hips off the floor so that your abs contract and your butt is no longer touching the ground.

Keep your chin tucked in to your chest.

Take SUNDAY off!

278

#217

pat yourself on the back

Congrats, you made it! Always make sure to reward yourself when completing any new workout. Your brain will connect the positive memory with the workout, and you'll want to keep doing it to get that same feeling!

the advanced workout

Get strong and fit with this head-to-toe routine from celeb fitness guru **Radu Teodorescu.** It's tough at first, but it will get easier—and it works!

Do 1 set of 6 to 8 reps **3 times a week** to start. Work your way up to 3 sets of 12 reps each, pausing for only 30 seconds between sets.

Warm up first. Rotate your neck and shoulders, and stretch arms and legs, holding each stretch for **5 seconds.** Then jog in place until you break a light sweat.

You'll need: 3-pound weights (or the heaviest you can handle) and a sturdy chair.

#218
plié squat with elevation

a. Hold the back of a chair for balance. Spread your legs wide and squat with your feet about two feet apart and your knees in line with your toes. Then stand up with your back straight and quickly rise up onto the tips of your toes. Return to starting position and repeat.

a.

b.

#219 sit-and-jump

a. Sit with your butt on the edge of a chair, hands resting on your knees.

b. Jump straight up in the air (but not out and away from the chair), raising your arms above your head. Sit back down and repeat.

283

a.

#220
leg hurdles

a. Get on all fours, then lift and bend your left knee out to the side.

b. Push back and up, leading with your heel, keeping toes flexed and leg high. Return to start and repeat for a full set, then switch legs.

b.

a.

b.

#221
seated tuck

a. With your legs extended in front of you, lean back slightly on the side of a chair.

b. Quickly tuck your legs into your chest, then slowly lower them so your feet just skim the floor. Repeat for a full set.

#222
balanced leg lifts

a. Hold your knees to your chest. Flex your feet by pulling your toes inward towards your shin.

b. Balance on your butt for 2 seconds as you stretch arms and point right foot up. Return to start; switch legs. Repeat 2 or 3 more times for a full set.

a.

b.

a.

b.

#223
sit-up and push-up

a. Sit in a V position with your arms raised straight up above your head

b. Twist at the waist, reach across your torso, lower yourself to the ground, and push up. Return to start. Repeat for a full set of reps, and then switch sides.

287

a.

#224

chair dips

a. Hold the edge of a chair with feet flexed and heels on the ground. (Prop chair against a wall.)

b. Bend elbows to lower your body down, almost to the floor. Push up with your arms to return to start and repeat.

b.

#225
weighted punches

a. Holding 3-to-5 pound weights against your chest stand with feet shoulder-width apart.

b. Quickly jab the air in front of you, alternating arms without locking elbows. Repeat for a full set.

#226 bicep curls

Slightly bend knees and hold weights at sides. Bend elbows, palms facing shoulders. Bend arms down and hold for 5 seconds, then return weights and hold. Repeat 10 reps.

a.

b.

#227
crossover kicks

a. Hold the back of a chair, with your right leg crossed behind you and left leg bent in front.

b. Push off your left leg to swing your right leg up as high as possible. Do 25 reps per leg daily and work up to 1 set of 100 to see results in 2 weeks! (No need to do multiple sets for this move.)

eat right, feel great!

With your **crazy-busy** life, avoiding junk food might seem impossible, but in the next chapter, you'll find everything you need to help you eat right without all of the stress: healthy ideas for breakfast, lunch, dinner, and snacks; smart choices on the go; and even what to order at your favorite restaurants. Get ready to **ditch** everything you ever learned about dieting, and start learning what to eat to make you **feel great** now!

The best way to stay healthy and happy is to practice good eating habits **every day!** This section will give you **tips and tricks** to keep in mind at school, at practice, and on the weekends with friends!

Health Tips!

#228
respect your body

Being good to yourself is the most important part of eating right. When you respect something you naturally want to treat it well, right? So the more you respect your body, the more you'll want to nourish it with the healthiest foods. Avoiding junk food becomes a whole lot easier because you're working with your body instead of fighting against it.

#229
know your preferences

Everybody has foods they like and dislike and schedules they do and don't like to follow. Forcing down broccoli even though it grosses you out isn't necessarily going to be good for your health if it just make you miserable. Try to find a balance between what you crave and what you know is best for your body!

#230
don't skip meals

Eat 3 meals and at least 1 snack every day. Just like a car, every part of your body needs fuel to run, so keep your engine revved up with regular balanced meals and snacks.

#231 make a pyramid

You've heard it a million times, but breakfast and lunch are much more important than dinner because they provide you with all your energy for the morning and afternoon. If you eat a big breakfast, a medium-size lunch, and a small dinner, you will be giving your metabolism exactly what it needs to burn all day!

#232
keep it balanced

Every time you eat, make sure you've built in protein (like meat, eggs, dairy products, tofu or beans), carbs (whole grains, rice, bread, vegetables and fruit), and healthy fats (olive oil, vegetable or canola oil, or trans-fat free spread). You can succeed by using this simple rule of thumb: Half your plate should be veggies, one-fourth should be carbs, and one-fourth should be protein. This combo burns at a steady rate so you'll stay full until your next meal.

#233
fill up on good fats

Not all fats are bad for you.
Monounsaturated fats (found in
avocadoes, nuts, canola oil and olive
oil) are great for your heart and may
even protect you against some cancers

#234
check for bad fats

Try to avoid trans fats. These are man-made fats that taste different than natural fats, don't spoil as quickly as vegetable or animal fats, and are often used in processed foods and could contribute to heart disease and diabetes. Look for products that say "trans-fat free" on the label.

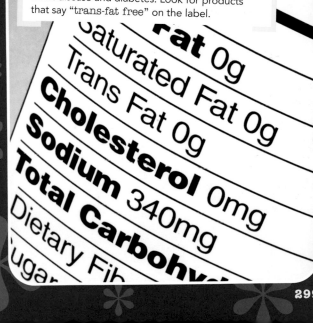

#235
limit saturated fat

Try to cut back on saturated fats—the kind found in butter and red meat, (many greasy foods, like fries, are fried in this type of fat). It can leave you feeling sluggish if you eat a lot of it.

#236
taste the rainbow

Get colorful with your plate. By eating at least 5 servings of fruits and veggies every day, you'll get in many of the vitamins and minerals your body needs to stay energized, fight off germs, and make sure your brain's on its fastest speed.

#237
drink your veggies

Feeling bloated? Try drinking low-sodium vegetable juice. Its high potassium content helps balance out extra sodium in the body (which can lead to bloat).

#238
forgo the junk

Junk food like soda, candy bars, and stuff from the vending machine has little actual nutrients, and usually contains a lot of sugar and trans fat, so just eat it in moderation. That means making it a once-in-a-while treat, rather than a daily habit.

#239
check your toppings

While dips, dressings, and spreads add a lot of flavor, they can also add a lot of fat and calories! next time you're spreading on the mayo, try to use just 1 teaspoon instead of a huge dollop.

#240
stay hydrated

Fill up on H_2O. Your body needs at least eight 8-oz glasses of water every day to flush out toxins, burn up food properly, and keep your skin clear, so drink up!

Nutrition Facts

Serving Size
Servings Per Container

Amount Per Serving

Calories
Calories from Fat

Total Fat
Saturated Fat
Trans Fat

Cholesterol

Sodium

Total Carbohydra
Dietary Fiber
Sugars

in

Daily Values are based
Your daily values ma
ding on your calorie n

Calories	2,000
Less than	65g
Less than	20g
Less than	300mg

#241
don't grab and go

It's hard to know how healthy your food really is, so that's why it's so important to read the labels. One key ingredient to avoid: High Fructose Corn Syrup—it's a man-made form of sugar found in many processed foods. It can spike your blood sugar which makes you feel light-headed, then tired, and could even lead to extra belly fat.

#242
bring on the vitamins

Load up on super-foods like blueberries, beans, and broccoli. They have tons of anti-oxidants to keep your body in Superwoman shape. They help your lungs breathe easier, your brain work faster and keep you from getting sick.

#243
boost your mind and body

Improve your memory and protect yourself from sports injuries by eating foods with Omega-3s—a type of nutrient found in wild salmon, walnuts and fortified eggs.

#244 nix a cold

Vitamin C has been shown to both keep colds away and help clear them up once they've started. Find it in citrus fruits, strawberries, and broccoli, and eat more if you are already sneezing!

#245
say okay to dairy

You've heard it a million times, but foods with calcium, like milk, cheese and yogurt keep your bones strong (important if you're always on the playing field!). Be sure to eat at least a serving a day.

#246
skimp on sweets

Sugary treats like cookies and ice cream taste so good, but too much sugar in your diet can make it harder to concentrate, and can lead to weight gain. Think of dessert as a special treat, and eat it just two or three times a week.

#247
pucker up

Want the very best snack around? Pink grapefruit has one of the highest concentrations of antioxidants. It's also packed with Vitamin C, which helps reduce insulin (blood sugar), which throw your body out of whack!

#248
choose wheat, not white

When building a meal, make whole grains the anchor. Whole grain cereals and breads, whole-wheat pasta, brown rice, barley, quinoa and other unprocessed grains make you feel fuller longer because they slow down digestion, and they contain a ton of great nutrients.

#249
snack smart.

Choose nuts over candy bars. They're another superfood packed with nutrients that are great for your heart—and can even rev your metabolism.

#250
have fruit for dessert

If you feel your sweet tooth kicking in after lunch or dinner, grab an apple, orange, or some strawberries! Fruit is tasty and has tons of nutrients, without refined sugar or fat!

#251 don't diet

Your body needs the proper amount of calories while it's still growing so if you're trying to lose weight, don't skip meals or try fad diets. Neither work long-term, because when you're hungry, or feel like you're depriving yourself, you'll be more likely to binge on unhealthy foods. Instead, go back to the basics: more fruits and veggies and normal portions.

#252
make your own portions

Restaurant portion sizes have become so huge, we end up eating double the amount we normally would. Sometimes you end up eating that way at home too, just out of habit. If you're ever faced with too-huge plate, eat half, stop, and see if you are still hungry. You might find you are full! That way you'll get used to going by your body's natural hunger signals.

#253
resist the habit

If you usually keep picking at an unfinished plate of food even after you're full, remind yourself to stop by covering it with your napkin.

#254
pay attention to hunger

Try "rating" your hunger. Using a scale of 1 to 5, try to put a number to how hungry you feel (1 being starving, 5 being stuffed). When you're feeling hungry, try to eat until you're in the 3–4 range. Keep practicing, and you'll start doing it all the time without thinking!

#255
when in doubt, drink

If you're hungry in between meals, you might actually be thirsty. Reach for water or tea before snacking and see if the drink satisfies you.

#256
skip meat sometimes

Go vegetarian every once in a while. Not only will you get great nutrients from all the vegetables you're eating, but you'll help cut down on the world's carbon footprint, since it takes way more greenhouse gasses to produce beef and dairy as it does veggies.

#257
limit the juice

Fruit juice may be super refreshing, but so are the fruits themselves, and they don't have refined sugar. Try substituting your morning glass of OJ with a small orange, and you might find you are even more satisfied.

#258 eat carbs

Forget about all of the anti-carb hype. Your brain and body need them to function. Just choose complex carbs (like whole grains, beans, fruits & veggies, and dairy products, etc.) over the simple carbs (candy, soft drinks, white bread, etc) since they don't contain any nutrients.

#259
go easy on java

Caffeine has been known to increase energy and make you feel more alert but too much can make you feel anxious and jittery, so try to stick to one or two cups a day.

#260

pack in the protein

Eat two servings of protein (like meat or tofu) each day, each about the size of a deck of cards. Protein keeps muscles, bones strong and healthy, and helps skin stay glowing.

#261

prepare for the game

The night before a sports meet, eat a meal with carbohydrates, fiber, and protein. A bowl of pasta with tomato sauce, veggies, and chicken has the right balance of slow-burning carbs and energy.

#262
fuel your brain

Have a big history test in the morning? Eat fish for dinner! Studies have shown that the omega-3 fatty acids found in fish like salmon may improve your brain's performance over time. Dark, leafy green veggies like spinach and arugula are also good for your memory, so be sure to have some salad, too!

#263
sit at the table

Try not to eat in front of the TV or computer. When you're paying attention to something other than the food in front of you, you're more likely to overeat. If you're not willing to turn off the tube, serve yourself before your show comes on so you can monitor your portion size.

#264
digest before bed

Always try to eat dinner at least 3 hours before going to sleep. This gives your body enough time to digest your last meal so you can sleep better.

#265
rock the red

Red peppers have twice as much Vitamin C and nine times as much Vitamin A as green ones. They help your body fight diseases like asthma and cancer, and can even improve your eyesight (great for becoming a sports star)! Puree them to make soup, or just slice them up raw for pre-dinner snack.

#266

grab the garlic

It may sound strange, but eating garlic could actually help keep your skin clear! It contains powerful anti-inflammatory ingredients, which help reduce redness and swelling. So chop up some cloves and throw them into stir-fries, soups, and pastas!

#267

go for ginger

Ginger is considered an herbal medicine that can prevent and help things like nausea and indigestion. Try adding raw ginger slices to your tea to soothe your stomachache!

#268
eat better, sleep better

Do you snore? Studies have shown that getting more zinc in you diet can help you sleep better at night! Some foods with high zinc levels include pumpkin seeds, non-fat yogurt, and spinach.

#269 breathe easier

Stuffed up? Eating spicy foods will help you clear out your nasal cavity! Dig into hot salsas and jalapeno peppers, or drizzle Tabasco sauce or cayenne pepper flakes on your food!

#270 grains

When serving yourself grains, think of index card—that's the correct portion.

#271 veggies

One serving of raw veggies is about the size of a baseball.

#272 juice

Since fruit or vegetable juice can be very high in sugar, make sure your portions are no more than 8 oz, about the size of your fist.

#273 dried fruit

Dried fruit like raisins and apricots are a great snack. One portion should be the size of an egg.

#274 fruit

A serving of raw fruit (canned, fresh, or frozen) is about the size of a pool ball.

#275

jam or jelly

Jams and jellies can be high in sugar and high-fructose corn syrup, so look for those containing only fruit and "pectin" (a solidifier) or just spread about one tablespoon full on your bread.

#276
berries
Three handfuls (or four tablespoons) of berries is the perfect portion.

#277
protein
Protein like beef, poultry, fish, or tofu should equal the size of a deck of cards.

#278
fruit

Whole fruit with the skin on, like nectarines, plums, apples, and bananas each come in the perfect portion size—no measuring needed!

#279 healthy fats

A healthy serving of heavy spreads like peanut butter, cream cheese, or hummus is 2 tablespoons, about the size of a golf ball.

breakfast, lunch, dinner, and snacks

Your body needs three healthy, balanced meals and one snack each day to feel its **absolute best**. Here's how to make them manageable, nutritious, and delicious!

Breakfast!

#280 wake up!

Make time for breakfast. A healthy meal revs your metabolism and gives you energy for the school day.

#281
fast food

At the drive-through, grab an egg sandwich with Canadian bacon. It's relatively low in fat, and has the right balance of carbs and protein to keep you feeling full until lunch.

#282
on the shelves

At the quickie-mart, grab an energy bar (like Lunabar) or fruit or yogurt to keep hunger in check.

#283
homemade

In too much of a hurry to eat at home? Pack a sandwich made from peanut butter and whole-wheat toast.

#284
eat right out

Out at the diner? Order two eggs sunny side up with toast and one slice of ham—a perfectly balanced meal.

#285

stick to healthy cereals

Cereal can be a great start to the day—just look for types without a ton of sugar (10 grams or less) and at least 5 grams of fiber like Kashi or you'll crash by lunchtime.

#286

go for grains

Look for the words whole grains on the box. That means the cereal contains more of the healthy parts of the wheat—the nutrients in whole grains are great for your hair and skin.

Kellogg's
Raisin Bran

2 REDUCED FAT MILK
VITAMIN A & D 2% MILKFAT
Less Fat Than Whole Milk
SEE SIDE FOR INFORMATION

#287
school time

At the caf, order any whole grain cereal (Raisin Bran, Total) with 2 percent or skim milk.

#288
avoid mega muffins

Many muffins you find in coffee shops contain almost half a day's worth of fat and calories, so make them a once in a while treat or just eat half.

#289
halve it

Bagels with cream cheese are usually double the amount of fat and cals you need for breakfast. In fact, bagels these days are so big that eating a whole one is like eating four pieces of bread! Cut yours in half.

#290
lighten up

Look for whipped cream cheese, which contains half the fat of the regular kind.

#291
no dough

Say no to doughnut holes—they pack in empty calories from sugar and little else, so you'll zone out by homeroom.

#292

less fat might mean more sugar

Even though reduced-fat muffins sound better for you, watch out. They are usually loaded with sugar to make up for the fat they're missing, which can just make you feel wired, then hungry again 20 minutes later.

#293
fill up with fruit

Breakfast is a great time to start
packing in the 5 servings of fruit and
veggies you need each day. Get your
fill by adding a banana or some
orange slices to breakfast.

#294
say yes to yogurt

Yogurt is a great source of calcium (good for pretty teeth and healthy bones), but stick to unsweetened low-fat type, since non-fat is usually sweetened with a ton of sugar to make up for the flavor.

#295

add crunchy to smooth

Sprinkle wheat germ or flaxseeds over your yogurt for a little crunch and a lot of health benefits! Wheat germ is packed with Vitamin E, which keeps your hair shiny, and flaxseeds have high levels of Omega-3 fatty acids.

#296
sip it

Fruit smoothies are a great breakfast as long as they're made with yogurt and fresh fruit. Just stop sipping when you feel full, since store-bought smoothies can be huge!

#297
scrambled or poached

Eggs are one of the best ways to start the day, since the protein will keep you going strong until lunch.

#298 fill'er up

Omelets are yummy and packed with lean protein—increase the nutri-factor by adding only veggie fillings, and stop when you're full since restaurant portions can be big.

#299
hold the homefries

When you're out at a breakfast place, try to order whole wheat toast instead of homefries. They're usually fried in a lot of grease, so if you get them, eat just a few.

#300
leggo my eggo

Frozen waffles are perfect for weekdays! Whole-wheat and multi-grain ones are filling and a great source of fiber.

#301
watch the toppings

Cut the unhealthy sugar and fats by using only a pat of butter and just a few spoonfuls of syrup to sweeten waffles—or better yet, add fiber with fresh or thawed frozen berries.

#302
do dairy

Calcium is good for your teeth, bones and nails, and even helps with PMS, so make sure you're getting at least 3–4 servings a day. Low-fat cottage cheese is a great source. Sweeten it up naturally by adding cantaloupe or fresh peaches.

#303
get wheat-y

Opt for whole-wheat pancakes if you can. They'll burn slowly (and you won't get that sugar-high feeling!).

#304
skip the yolk

Make your omelets with egg whites. They are low in saturated fat and contain less cholesterol than a whole egg.

#305
healthier fraps

Frosty blended coffee drinks taste so good, but they can contain a whole meal's worth of fat and calories. Order the smallest size and substitute low-fat or non-fat milk if possible.

#306 fruit fix

Just one cup of blackberries can give you half of your daily serving of Vitamin C! Add these sweet berries to your cereal in the morning.

#307

limit the griddle treats

Pancakes aren't the healthiest breakfast (the refined carbs make your blood sugar spike and then crash, leaving you tired), so stick to a plateful just a few times a month.

#308

eat your oats

Oatmeal is packed with fiber—it'll keep you full and focused until lunch.

#309
the right java

Your best latte bets are a tall skim latte from Starbucks, or a small Latte Lite from Dunkin' Donuts.

#310

quench your thirst

Try iced tea when you're craving a cold Starbucks fix. Go for a tall iced passion or green shaken iced tea lemonade—they're sweet, refreshing, and contains half the cals of Fraps!

Lunch!

#311
the lunch of champions

Want to stay awake in class after lunch? Choose a meal with a mix of lean protein, carbs and veggies, and little unhealthy fats— like a ham sandwich, apple and a bite-sized Hershey's miniature!

#312
midday don't

Try to avoid typical caf fare like fries, breaded chicken fingers and pizza, since they can contain a lot of unhealthy grease and little nutrients.

#313 on the go

Yes, it's fast, but most drive-through food is packed with unhealthy trans fat. Stick with a grilled chicken sandwich or small hamburger and skip the fries.

#314 on the shelves

Most food at the convenience store is prepackaged, prepared and packed with chemicals—stick with a frozen bean burrito, and supplement with a piece of fruit if they have it.

#315
homemade

Have a little more time to make
something from scratch? Grab a
wrap and fill it with hummus,
low-fat shredded cheese,
lettuce and other veggies. It's
low-fat, quick and full of fiber.

#316 at school

Choices in the à la carte lines at the caf are usually pretty unhealthy—the food is loaded with grease and salt. Stick to the stuff in the regular lines, like chili—it has to meet nutrition standards—the beans pack in fiber and protein to keep you full the rest of the day.

#317
bring your own healthy sides

Since caf sandwiches usually just include bread and meat, get in the fiber you need to stay fuller longer by adding fruit like grapes or veggies, such as carrots and celery sticks.

#318 watch the chips

Chips are a typical sandwich side order, but since they're usually fried in saturated fats, try to eat just a few. Baked chips are just as delicious and are lower in fat and calories.

#319 yummy treat

Make your PB&J with whole-wheat bread, banana and strawberries, and low-sugar strawberry preserves. The healthy carbs (fresh fruit and high-fiber bread) make this version less sugary and more filling than your standard PB&J!

#320 sip on soup

Soup is another great lunch pick—it's hearty and filling, and usually contains loads of veggies, protein, or beans. Just pick broth over creamy, since it can be loaded with extra fat.

#321
make it mexican

Typical turkey sammies can get boring, but salsa adds spice and avocado has the richness of mayo (but with healthier fats)!

#322
bigger and better

Enjoy a honey ham sandwich made with lettuce and tomato on rye bread. When paired with Sunchips and a Diet Coke, this whole lunch has the same number of cals as just a medium side order of fast-food fries.

#323
very veggie

When you hit up the salad bar, choose power-veggies like tomatoes, chickpeas, carrots, olives, and cucumber. They make your salad tasty and are packed with vitamins, nutrients and filling fiber too!

#324
diner dos

At the diner, ask for a turkey sandwich. It's your best choice because it has lean protein and some veggies.

#325
grilled, not fried

Choose grilled bbq chicken over chicken fingers to cut most of the fat.

#326 super subs

Want take-out? Grab a 6-inch turkey sandwich from Subway for a boost of lean protein that will keep you full all afternoon.

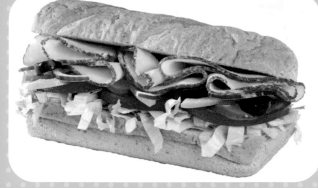

#327 best burgers

Hamburgers aren't bad as a once-in-a-while lunch—but try to substitute 94% ground sirloin, which is lower in fat than regular ground beef.

#328
stay small

When you're grabbing lunch at a fast-food place, stick to the smallest-size burger.

#329
take-away tuna

Tuna salad is a lunch staple, but most deli versions pack in unhealthy mayo, so keep it to only once in a while. You can also make your own tuna using non-fat, plain yogurt, or reduced-fat mayo.

#330
try tortilla

Baked tortilla chips are a great chip substitute, because they contain less fat and calories than regular chips.

#331
very veggie

At the make-your-own salad place, try to choose more veggie add-ins over cheese, which can be high in fat.

#332 pretzels please

Pretzels are an okay side, too, just make sure the ingredients don't contain chemicals you can't pronounce or high-fructose corn syrup.

#333 pick popcorn

Popcorn can also be a great side—the corn has thiamin, which is great for your brain. Just look for plain, or a kind flavored naturally with real cheese and olive or canola oil, instead of chemicals.

#334
slimmer sides

Serve up a side of guac or salsa with your chips instead of prepackaged dip and you'll fit in heart-healthy fats and Omega-6s.

#335
vinaigrettes are best

Creamy dressings taste yummy, but can take your salad from healthy to harmful, so steer clear of anything white, like ranch, or blue cheese.

#336
be careful with ceasar

Most Caesar salad has dressing made with anchovies—a great source of omega-6 fatty acid, but try to have a side portion only, since the cheese and dressing make this classic salad slightly heavier.

#337
healthy pies

Stick to veggie toppings on your pizza, such as onions, peppers, and mushrooms, rather than meat, such as pepperoni or sausage— they contain a lot of fat and preservatives.

#338

an italian panini

Eggplant has powerful ingredients that help your body fight diseases. For a yummy vegetarian sandwich, put grilled eggplant slices, basil, and some low-fat mozzarella cheese on toasted multi-grain bread.

#339
healthier fries

French fries are okay, but try to find oven-baked kinds, since the ones fried in oil have twice the fat.

#340
a little cheese

Cheese on burgers can add additional unhealthy saturated fat, so use only a slice.

#341
cut the cream

Cream soups contain a lot of saturated fats, so eat them only once in a while. Broth soups like chicken noodle and minestrone are packed with healthy veggies and very little calories.

#342

pick your pizza

Pizza can be a great lunch, if you stick to one 6" slice. Try to find thin-crust, or whole-wheat versions for added fiber.

#343
lean protein

Load up your salad with low-fat fiber (from veggies) and protein, in the form of chickpeas, red and black beans, or grilled chicken breast.

#344
broil, don't fry

Grilled cheese sandwiches are usually fried in butter, but you can skip the grease by making this healthy version: Mist outside of the bread with cooking spray, then put it in a sandwich press or under the broiler.

#345

mix it up

Instead of cheese and crackers as an appetizer, try hummus and pita. It has tons of flavor, but less fat.

#346

pick poultry

Chicken breast is a great source of low-fat protein, but choose grilled chicken over deep-fried—too much grease.

#347 brown is best

Whole-grain bread packs in more fill-you-up fiber—white or sub rolls aren't the best picks since they contain a lot of extra empty calories.

Dinner!

#348

have a nice dinner

If you sit down to eat it with your family, studies show you'll be less likely to eat overeat.

#349
vary your meats

Most days you should pick low-fat protein like chicken, turkey or fish. But once or twice a week it's fine to eat a steak. It has iron your body needs!

#350
perfect pasta

Whole-wheat pasta primavera balances carbs and veggies to keep you satisfied.

#351 lighter lasagna

Instead of lasagna made with ground beef, use ground turkey and tons of veggies to shave fat and calories without sacrificing taste.

#352

take it easy with takeout

Takeout favorites like Chinese food or Thai can be loaded in unhealthy grease—try to eat just a half portion, and supplement it with a broth-based soup starter.

#353 asian fusion

Grilled chicken teriyaki with a cup of brown rice and steamed veggies is a great dinner choice. The protein/carb combo slowly burns, keeping you full and focused during homework time.

#354
tasty tortillas

For a spicy chicken dinner, roll up shredded chicken in flour tortillas, cover them in salsa and put them in the oven until they're warm and sizzling.

#355
turkey dinner

Oven-roasted turkey breast is a great source of lean protein, and it contains powerful mood-regulating hormones that can make you happier.

#356
opt for oil

At home, make the suggestion that your family switch from cooking with butter to olive oil or canola oil. You'll hardly taste the difference and your food will be lighter, healthier and packed with good-for-you omega-3s.

#357 say salmon

Salmon with wild rice combines Omega-3 fatty acids and Vitamin D with slow-burning carbs—perfect when you need to stay focused at night.

#358

salmon suggestions

If plain cooked salmon alone is too fishy tasting to you, try it grilled with soy sauce, or poached.

#359
way to go white

White, flaky fish like cod or haddock is a great source of selenium, which fights cancer, and keeps your brain working hard for study-time.

#360
slimmer steak

Lean sirloin is lower in fat than other steak cuts, so choose it or a filet when ordering instead of the high-fat ribeyes or New York Strips.

#361
fabulous fajitas

Steak fajitas are a healthy Tex-Mex meal, since they're grilled, not fried, and contain veggie and bean add-ins for extra fiber.

#362 take it slow

It takes 20 minutes for our stomachs to let our brain know we're full, so try to eat slowly to avoid that too-full feeling.

#363 on the side

Watch out for sides that usually accompany turkey, like mashed potatoes with gravy and stuffing, which can be very fattening. Load on the cranberry sauce instead and you'll get antioxidants without the fat!

#364
bring on the broc

Broccoli is a veggie powerhouse, containing tons of Vitamins C and K, which keep your body at the top of its game.

#365
the sweeter the better

Try swapping the regular baked potato for a sweet potato. It's high in beta carotene which in your body converts to vitamin A, which keeps you from getting sick.

#366

brave the brussels

Brussels sprouts contain vitamin K and folate, which keep your muscles working hard.

#367 snag a salad

If you're starving for dinner, ask for a small salad with vinaigrette dressing instead of reaching for bread—it is packed with nutrients and won't fill you up too much before the main course comes.

#368 eat your leaves

Greens, like collard greens, spinach and okra contain Beta-carotene, a super healthy antioxidant which helps you think more clearly.

#369
side-dish suggestions

Stick to side dishes that are steamed, baked, or boiled, like an ear of corn or green beans. This way you will get more nutrients without all the grease.

#370 leave the skin

When making boiled or mashed potatoes, leave the skin on! It contains way more nutrients than the inside!

#371 go red

Want to increase your meal's health factor? Add tomatoes! They've got lycopene and its better absorbed by your body when its cooked with olive oil.

#372

cobs or kernels

Corn is a great side dish for any dinner plate. It's full of thiamin, which increases your energy and boosts your brain power!

#373
dark green is great

The best type of salad is made from dark, leafy veggies. Romaine, Bibb, and arugula are all great examples, containing lots of Vitamin-K—a must for strong bones. Ask your parents to replace iceberg lettuce (which is mostly filled with water) with these nutrient-rich versions.

#374
make it mushrooms
These little wonders from the fungi family help you digest food better.

#375

pizza pizza

Instead of ordering in, try making your own pizza at home! Just top individual English muffins with tomato sauce, mozzarella cheese, and olives, peppers, or mushrooms, and heat everything in the oven.

Snacks!

#376
start snacking

The right snacks keep you functioning full-steam ahead throughout the day. Look for bars that contain more than 2 grams of fiber so you feel fuller longer.

#377 on the go

At the fast-food place, choose apple dippers or carrot sticks over the snack-size sandwiches, and get a boost of vitamins.

#378
on the shelves

At the convenience store, look for a snack with the lowest number of ingredients on the package to avoid unhealthy sugar- or trans-fat loaded snacks. Pretzels or almonds can be good options.

#379
a peck of peppers

Cut up red pepper strips are your best friend if you're on a sports team. They contain the chemical lycopene which helps you last longer when exercising.

#380
at school

At the caf, treats like cheese fries can contain a few days' worth of fat and calories—stick to whole fruit, when possible, or hit up the vending machine for a granola bar or baked chips.

#381
can the cans

Stay away from packaged fruits like canned peaches and pears; the juice they are preserved in has lots of high-fructose corn syrup. If you're looking for a quick fruit fix, grab some dried cranberries, dried apricots, or raisins.

#382
pop your own corn

Use an air popper to pop some popcorn with no oil. Bring it in a plastic baggie, or microwave a small bag of light popcorn at school for a low-cal, fiber-filled snack that tastes just as good as chips.

#383 pick peanuts

While they're both loaded in sugar, peanut M&M's are a better option than regular, since the protein in the nuts can help slow the sugar spike from the candy.

#384
best bars

If your stomach's already growling midmorning, a calorie-controlled snack bar like (Special K) is a great portable snack to tide you over until lunch—just look for ones under 150 calories, so you're not eating too much sugar.

#385
fresh fruit

Fruit salad can be very healthy, or very unhealthy—just look for the kind found at delis or supermarkets, made up of fresh-cut whole fruit—and skip the kind in a can, since it can contain a dessert portion's worth of sugary syrup as a sweetener.

#386
boost brain power

Want to ace the test? Blue, red, and purple-y colored foods like raspberries and blue-berries contain chemicals that make your brain respond better to incoming info!

#387
super spreads

Health food stores like Whole Foods let you make your own all-natural peanut and almond butter. Spread some on a rice cake for the perfect afternoon snack at home that's loaded with protein and healthy fats.

#388
careful with crackers

Peanut-butter crackers from the vending machine actually contain an unhealthy amount of trans fat—stick with them as a once-in-a-while treat, rather than an everyday habit.

#389
try triscuits

Triscuits are just as tasty, but these delicious squares contain more fiber and less sugar than other crackers.

#390

awesome appetizers

Crackers are a great pre-dinner snack, but read the label to make sure to avoid types that are made with hydrogenated (fake) oils and high-fructose corn syrup.

#391
a helping of hummus

Hummus spread on toasted pieces of fiber-filled whole-wheat pita will keep you full until dinner.

#392 chips and dip

Low-fat tortilla chips with fiber-rich black beans and lycopene-full (meaning heart-healthy!) salsa is a great mid-afternoon snack!

#393

pudding for dessert

After dinner, choose your pudding wisely!
Look for sugar-free labels: manufacturers
often add a ton of sugar when taking
out the fat.

#394
nuts for nuts

Nuts are a convenient snack option—keep almonds, cashews, and walnuts on hand for a crunchy and filling source of protein.

#395 a fun-dae

Create another fun and low-fat after-dinner treat by crushing up a graham cracker and layering it with low-fat pudding and light whipped cream.

#396 think thin

Frozen pizza is a great late-night meal, but instead of the "snack" frozen pizza options, like Hot Pockets, munch on a slice of the thin-crust frozen regular topped with veggies, for an extra boost of nutrients and less greasy cheese.

#397

dig into dried grapes

Most sweet treats are bad for your teeth, but raisins actually contain a phytochemical that prevents cavities. A box of raisins is perfect for a quick and sweet dessert!

#398
spice it up

You know that head rush feeling you get after you eat a lot of sugar? Top your sweets with cinnamon and you'll slow down digestion, which causes the energy spike.

#399
don't ditch cookies

But, stick to made-from-scratch cookies, and add in healthy nuts and dried fruit for an even better treat!

#400
s'more of that

Believe it or not, you can make healthy s'mores from low-sugar graham crackers, a marshmallow, and chocolate, microwaved for 15 seconds.

NEW! JELL-O with Antioxidants*

6 SNACKS

strawberry acai

Sugar Free | 10 Calories

LOW CALORIE GELATIN SNACKS • *GOOD SOURCE OF VITAMINS A & E

#401

nutritious sweets

Look for no-sugar jello, like Jello Fruit Passions, which in addition to being a low-cal treat actually counts as a serving of fruit, too!

#402
cookie tips

Cookies such as ginger snaps, Nestle chocolate chip cookie dough, and graham crackers all have little trans fat, and contain less sugar than other cookies.

#403
skip the shelves

Choose wisely with store-bought since most chocolate, candy and cookies an contain saturated fat, and loads of sugar.

#404
be careful with ice cream

When sizing up ice-cream competition, check the label carefully—some "light" brands have more fat, calories, and sugar than regular lines.

#405
double churned and delicious

Words to watch for: "double-churned." It means the ice-cream is made with skim milk, whipped with a lot of air, so it tastes creamy, but is actually lower in fat.

#406
ice pops, please

For other frozen treats, stick to popsicles! They do contain sugar, but the rest is water and fruit—and they last a long time!

#407 ice-cream bars

Gooey ice-cream treats like Klondike and Snickers should be limited to being eaten every once in a while, since they contain the same blend of unhealthy fats and sugar as regular ice cream.

#408
stock up on sorbet

Ice-cream is a yummy dessert, but if you find yourself eating it every day, switch to fruit sorbet, which has fewer calories, and sometimes the nutrients and fiber of fruit, so you're not just eating empty sugar calories!

#409
yummy yogurt

Replace a sundae-sized bowl of ice-cream with fat-free soft-serve yogurt and you could eat it for four days for the same amount of calories!

#410
make your own fro-yo

For an even lower-calorie version of frozen yogurt, stick a light yogurt like Dannon or Yoplait in the freezer and enjoy it when it's frozen.

on the go

It can be hard to stick to good eating habits when you're not at home, especially with **temptations** lurking everywhere you go! The following tips will show you how to choose healthy over junky anywhere you go!

#411
hit up the H$_2$O

Choose water over soda—yes, the caffeine will keep you going through last period, but all that sugar is just extra calories you don't need. Studies showed teens who drink soda every day put on an average of 15 pounds a year.

#412

skip hot lunch

Skip the "snack bar" foods in favor of real food. Stuff on the snack bar—fries, chicken fingers—are usually fried in unhealthy oils, and you end up missing out on the fruit and vegetable servings you need to keep your mind and body working well.

#413
not just dessert

Don't replace meals with sweets. It seems smart—eat the same amount of cals you would and satisfy your sweet tooth—but skipping meals will just make you hungrier later on.

#414
special, please

Go for the special of the day—usually it's a meal containing the right mix of protein, veggies and carbs, which will help you think more clearly in class later. French bread pizza, bagels and cream cheese or chips won't give you the nutrition you need.

#415
at the quickie mart

Choose snacks wisely. The general rule is to look for stuff made with ingredients you can pronounce.

#416
the right mix

Snack mix containing pretzels, popcorn and dried fruit can be a good choice. Just look for the kind without too much extra candy.

#417
snap, crackle, and pop

Rice Krispie bars are a great snack, since the bulk of it is made with airy cereal, rather than sugar.

#418
healthy hydration

Thirsty? Avoid juice drinks, sweetened waters, and soda (even diet). They all contain high fructose corn syrup or other forms of added sugar, so pass them up for regular water, unsweetened iced tea or even low fat milk to save all the non-nutrient cals!

#419
add some zing

Instead of drinking lemonade and all the sugar that comes with it, just add 2 slices of lemon to a glass of flat water. Way zestier, but with zero cals!

420 go green

Green tea, that is. This beverage is full of antioxidants that help speed up your metabolism and prevent cancer. It has no calories and is a nice alternative to coffee when you need a little jolt of energy.

#421

use smaller plates!

It may sound strange, but we're eating bigger portions than ever and using a small plate will help you recognize how to stop when you're full—the best way to know you're eating the right amount.

#422

get your zs

Go to sleep earlier. Of course there's always someone to Facebook, but getting 8–9 hours of sleep will help stop you from overeating just for extra energy when you're exhausted.

#423 slow down

Spend at least 15 minutes eating any meal. That's how long it takes for the body to register that it's full, so if you scarf down food quickly, you might end up overeating. To help you slow down, try placing the fork down between each bite.

eat right, feel great!

#424
make it yourself

Avoid "opening packages" to eat. For example, try making a big salad for lunch, asking mom for grilled chicken or baked potato loaded with veggies for dinner, rather than anything you have to unwrap, like takeout.

#425
perfect portions

Remember the ¼, ¼, ½ rule: a fourth of your plate should have meat, a fourth some type of carb, and the rest should be veggies.

#426

close your chomper

Don't talk with food in your mouth—yes, it's more polite, but you'll also eat slower, and your body will register that you're full.

#427
schedule time to eat

It can be tricky to make good decisions when you're running around all day and night, so each morning, take a minute to map out the day, and what healthy options might be available to you at each meal time. It'll help you when you're in the moment and feeling rushed.

Out to Eat!

#428
wonderful wraps

This tasty slimmed-down sandwich has little saturated fat and no trans fat, but the sweet chili sauce makes it full of flavor.

Schlotzsky's Asian Chicken Wrap

460

Sbarro

#429
italian eats

While the thick-crust pizza here serves up a days worth of fat and cals alone, the veggie version cuts back on some of the cheese, slimming it down. If you eat here often, stick to the caprese or side salads and split a slice with a friend.

Dairy Queen

#430
scream for ice cream

Save the Blizzards for once-in-a-while and stick to the low-fat soft serve with strawberry topping, made with real strawberries.

#431 tex mex

Chipotle's a great healthy option, since all of its meat products were raised as humanely as possible, and never given any antibiotics, or growth hormones. The steak bowl is packed with protein and fiber!

Chipotle

#432
chinese choices

Panda Express

Thai Cashew Chicken has loads of fresh veggies, non-fried chicken, heart-helping cashews along with a light soy sauce. It's incredibly healthy and delicious compared to usually fried food.

#433

choose chicken

Give Chick-Fil-A an A+! It's removed all trans fats from the entire menu, and many of its items are great low-fat choices, including this Chargrilled Chicken and Fruit Salad!

Chick-Fil-A

#434

no big macs

A six-piece Chicken McNuggets is in the healthy calorie range for a meal, as is the Honey Mustard Snack Wrap, and the plain hamburger—just avoid the fat-loaded fries.

McDonald's

Cinnabon

#435
sweet splurge

Gooey cinnamon buns are super
tempting after a day of shopping
at the mall, but even though
they seem statisfying, the sugar-
and white-carb–filled treats can
put you into sugar shock.
Make it a once-in-a-while treat,
or split one with a bunch of
friends over iced coffees!

Starbucks

VIVANNO™
ishing blends

#436
super smoothie

Vivannos contain a whole banana, fiber powder, milk, and real juice making them the perfect balanced snack.
It's high in calories so sip until you feel full.

Taco Bell

#437
tasty tacos

Hard-shell tacos and refried meat and beans give the Bell a bad name, its lighter Fresco line all contains grilled meat or veggies, fiber-filled beans, and lower-in-fat shells making them the healthy menu choice.

#438

snag a sandwich

This hand-made sandwich chain has tons of great options—lean protein fixings like turkey, ham and roast beef, fresh-baked breads and lighter condiment choices, or switch it up with one of the soups.

Subway

Panera

#439 pick panera

This chain uses antiobiotic-free chicken, organic and all-natural produce and no trans-fats—so eat away, but watch portion size (stop eating when you're full). The perfect meal: low-fat vegetarian black bean soup and Mediterranean Veggie Sandwich.

#440
quick quiznos

Like Subway, it's not so hard to find something healthy here—just order lean-meat deli classics like turkey or ham, and go lighter on cheese and dressing toppings.

quiznos

Cosi

#441
careful with cosi

Even though they have whole grains, two slices of Cosi's homemade bread have the same amount of calories as a Big Mac! Instead of a sandwich, order the three-bean chili and banana parfait.

Burger King

#442
basics at burger king

Just like with the rest of
the burger chains, leave
the over-sized burgers
alone, and stick to single-
patty varieties with no
cheese or mayo.

Wendy's

#443
when at wendy's

Stick to the basics—a single burger with ketchup, not mayo, or a small chili, and you won't leave with that overstuffed, heartburn-y feeling.

#444
cut the crisp

Extra crispy means fried in extra grease, so try to eat just one or two pieces, or choose Crispy Strips or Original Recipe Grilled Chicken instead, and fill out your meal with mashed potatoes and gravy and a veggie side.

KFC

#445
spring for splitting

Salsa and guac are great, but chips that come with them are usually fried, so try to split one serving with the whole table.

#446
find the fajitas

As for main dishes, fajitas, since they're grilled with very little extra fat, make the best choice. Just stop eating once you're full, since portion sizes usually run x-large for that sizzling effect!

Tex-Mex

477

Chinese

#447
simply steamed

Choose steamed dumplings filled with veggies, chicken, or pork, over fried wontons or egg rolls.

#448
keep the kung pao

Since sesame chicken, orange chicken and General Tso's chicken all come dipped in unhealthy batter and then fried, choose Kung Pao chicken, which offsets a bit of the grease with fiber-filled veggies.

#449
healthier home fries

Home fries are okay—
that is if they're baked,
not fried. Otherwise,
they've got as much oil
as a plate of french fries.

At the Diner

#450
pass on pancakes

Like we mentioned earlier,
a short stack of syrup-y
pancakes is tasty, but the
surge of quick-burning
carbohydrates spikes your
blood sugar and signals
your body to start storing
fat. Instead, choose a
veggie-loaded omlette,
soup or a BLT.

Italian

#451 caprese please

Most of the time, stick with tomato and mozzarella caprese salads over Caesar, which is often loaded with high-in-fat creamy dressing, cheese, and croutons.

#452
pass the pomodoro

Order spaghetti pomodoro, which means fresh sauce and tomato. Creamy white sauces like alfredo can contain a full day's worth of fat and cals, so save for once-in-a-while.

#453
make it marinara

Order marinara sauce whenever it's an option—on pasta, as a dipping sauce, or on a sandwich. It's almost completely fat-free and has tons of lycopene.

#454 try tandoori

Indian's tricky, so stick with the word tandoori—
which means baked in a hot clay oven, rather
than stir-fried in oil, making it a healthy dinner

Indian

#455 no coconut

Skip dishes that are made with coconut milk,
a thick liquid that's very high in saturated fats.
Just one cup contains a whopping 552 calories!

#456
choose curry

Look for anything with "curry" in the title—it contains turmeric known to help your body digest food more efficiently!

Japanese

#457
simply sushi

Sushi rolls made from fresh, raw
fish and other fixings rolled in rice,
are lean, low-fat, high in protein
and great for your brain power.

#458
light and healthy

Japanese menus offer some of the healthiest offerings of any ethnic food restaurant—enjoy edamame (steamed soy beans), miso soup, or salad with ginger dressing to start.

#459
savor seafood

Fresh fish and other types of seafood have some excellent health benefits—the fats in oilier fish can help prevent everything from diabetes to cancer. Shellfish like shrimp, clams and crab contain calcium and protein, which strengthen bones and teeth.

Seafood

#460 forget the fried

Just look for steamed, grilled, broiled or baked varieties, since frying can add a lot more fat and calories.

Classic American

#461 skimp on dip

Go easy on "special sauce," like blue cheese dressing, and buffalo sauce. They all up the calorie and fat content to above-average. Choose ketchup or mustard instead.

#462 "fried" salads

Cobb, chef, and fried buffalo-chicken salads all contain the same amount of calories as a Big Mac. Stick to a mix of nutrient-rich dark greens, fresh veggies, and lean protein like shrimp or chicken.

BBQ

#463
taste of the south

BBQ joints are notorious for slow-roasting the fattiest cuts of meat, and pairing them with heavy, sugar-sweetened sides. Skip the pork and have pulled chicken doused in bbq sauce, baked beans, and collard greens which makes a well-balanced meal.

#464
splurges for sometimes

Once-in-a-while options include mac 'n' cheese, or hush puppies, since they're usually high in a mix of fat, calories, sugar, salt, and empty carbs!

Buffet

#465
chicken and veggies

Go for the rotisserie chicken with soup and steamed veggies or a small salad on the side.

#466
don't overdo it

Buffets can be tricky, since it's all about eating two or three platefuls. Try to pick just a small spoonful of everything you want to eat, to keep portions smaller.

#467 slim options

Your leanest choices at a buffet include carved meat like turkey or ham, salads with vinaigrette dressing and frozen yogurt for dessert.

#468
less of the heavy

When you're choosing sides at a buffet, take only a little bit of the cheesy, baked entrees like mac 'n' cheese and baked stuffed pasta, since they can be high in fat.

#469
slow down

Remember, you can always go up for more at a buffet, so take only what looks good and eat slowly to avoid that overly-full feeling.

#470 movie munchies

Movie-theatre popcorn tastes so yummy, but the processed butter adds about as much fat and cals as you need for the whole day! Share a small bag with a friend, skip the butter.

Around town!

#471
craving candy

Get a York Peppermint Patty
or junior mints and share—
they're relatively low in fat and
cals.

#472
hot diggity dog

At a sporting event, load a hotdog with the works—onions, ketchup, mustard and relish for a filling treat. All-beef franks are best, but even in a pinch, the processed pork kind still top nachos.

#473
pick peanuts

At the ballpark, peanuts in the shell are great— you get the monounsaturated (heart-healthy fats), plus the shells take a little longer to crack open, so you're not popping as many.

On a date!

#474 why not share

Don't stress— you're enjoying yourself! Pick what's looking best, and offer to split it—it's fun to share, and you won't get that overly full feeling!

#475
ditch dairy

You might want to pass on dairy, when you're on a date, since milk, cheese and iced cream can make you feel bloated and gassy.

#476
skip soda

Rethink the diet soda on a date. When the sweeteners in this drink break down in your stomach they give off gas—which you definitely don't want!

#477
forget the fries

Cheese fries are a big no-no; while it's fun to share, the extra grease can weigh you down and make you feel tired because your body has to work hard to digest it.

With friends!

#478

stop at "full"

It's fun to bond with friends over junk food, but it can make you feel less than stellar afterward. Rule of thumb: eat what you want, but stop when you get that first "I don't want to eat any more" feeling.

#479
no pressure

If you don't want to eat what everyone's eating, don't feel guilt, just say, "this, [fill in the blank] is sooooo good, but I'm just feeling too full right now." Your friends will move on to a new subject in a few seconds.

#480
help choose

If you're vegetarian and your whole crew keeps making you go to meat-centric restaurants, don't stress, or complain. Just research a few great places that offer a variety of options, and suggest them next time so no one in your group feels like they're getting short-changed.

#481
keep a schedule

Eat regular meals—it can be harder to eat healthily when you're snacking on treats throughout the day, so build a healthy base of breakfast, lunch, and dinner, and you'll be less tempted to over-do it on fun foods.

#482 hit the H_2O

Drink plenty of water. If you're in a sunny, warm climate, you might become dehydrated. Our bodies often think we're hungry, when often times, we're really just thirsty!

#483

sno-cones

Shaved ice contains sugar, but way less than most other boardwork treats. Plus, the cold treat lasts for ever.

SN
CO

#484

have fun on vacay

Eat what you want—it's vacation(!), but try eat only until you start to feel full—that means with greasier stuff like fried dough, it may only be a few bites—but hey, you're getting to have it, right?

#485
split for sure

Don't be afraid to split stuff at restaurants or speak up—most chains know their portions are huge, and want to make sure you're happy.

#486
fruit for you

The snack bar has the best summer food, but sometimes it's not so healthy. Treats you can eat every day? Try a fresh fruit cup.

#487

occasional ice cream

Instead of a daily ice-cream cone, mix it up with fruit bars—you'll save fat and calories, and get in a serving of nutrient-loaded fruit.

#488

a sprinkle of fun

when choosing ice-ceam toppings relatively low-in-cal sprinkles make a better choice than candy-bar toppings.

#489
get it grilled

Summertime food can go right or wrong fast—grilling is one of the healthiest way to cook, so stick to plenty of grilled chicken, steak, fish and veggies.

#490
grill go-tos

The healthiest pic on the grill menu? The grilled chicken sandwich—ask for bbq sauce or teriyaki sauce to add flavor without too many cals.

#491
bbq basics

Since burgers and hot dogs can contain a lot of saturated fat, try to eat them only a few times a week.

#492
at the lakeside bbq

Stick to healthy sides like bean salad, over chips, and potato salad made with mayo, which tip the meal too heavily on fat.

#493
safe seafood

Seafood is a summertime favorite, but try to choose the fried variety only once-in-a-while. Grilled, boiled, steamed, or baked is okay for every day!

#494
start with soup

Skip the bread basket. When you haven't eaten after a long day of sight seeing, you might be tempted to fill up fast on bread, which just adds empty calories. Instead, order a soup to start to get in servings of veggies you may have missed out on earlier in the day.

#495

marvelous melon

Watermelon, a summer favorite is loaded with vitamin A and C, which helps your body ward off infection, and keeps you hydrated!

#496
blended beverages

Smoothies are a great way to cool off in the summer. Just stick to non-fat plain yogurt or milk, crushed ice, and fresh fruit and skip the sugar-y fruit juices to keep it full of vitamins and low in extra calories your body doesn't need.

Holiday time!

December 2009

	1	2	3	4	5
6	7	8	9	10	11	12
13	14	15	16	17	18	19
20	21	22	23	24	25	26

#497
ho, ho, healthy

Come holiday time, most people start indulging on Thanksgiving and end New Year's Day! To overset a few days of overeating, plan to make healthy choices the rest of the month.

#498
dessert do's

As for holiday desserts, pumpkin pie can be healthy! The pumpkin contains beta-carotene, which is good for your eyes and skin, but stick to the true portion: 2" of crust!

#499
don't be a cookie monster

Holiday cookies and treats are always around, so stick to this strategy: have one cookie, but choose the one that looks yummiest and savor it. That way you won't feel deprived, and won't get that too-full feeling.

#500 definitely dark

If you have a choice between cakes, pies or a chocolate treat, choose the dark stuff. Chocolate, especially dark chocolate, is loaded with anti-oxidants, chemicals that prevent disease! And it's known to lift your mood.

index

index

Workout(s)

photo credits

special thanks

Ramona Braganza, www.ramonabraganza.com

Jarett Del Bene, www.workoutwithjarett.com

Vivica Jenkins

Gregory Joujon-Roche, www.onebodyonelife.com, *One Body, One Life* (Dutton, 2006)

Kathy Kaehler, www.kathykaehlerfitness.com, *Kathy Kaehler's Celebrity Workouts* (Broadway, 2004)

Jamie King, www.jamiekingofficial.com, *Rock Your Body* (Rodale, 2007)

Natasha Kufa, www.nk-evolutionbody.com

Cyndi Lee, www.omyoga.com/cyndi, *Yoga Body, Buddha Mind* (Riverhead, 2004)

Harley Pasternak, www.harleypasternak.com/about.html, *5-Factor Fitness* (Meredith, 2004)

Cindy Percival

Candice Richardson, teenyfitness.com/index.php

Keli Roberts, www.keliroberts.com, *Keli Roberts Fitness Hollywood* (Summit, 1997)

Bobby Strom, bobbystromfitness.com

Radu Teodorescu, *Radu's Simply Fit* (Andrews Mcmeel, 1996)

Jason Walsh, www.jasonwalshtraining.com

Mari Winsor, www.winsorfit.com, *The Pilates Powerhouse* (Da Capo, 1999)